WHAT THE MEDIA ARE SAYING

"Harley Gordon's book is bound to save American families untold anguish as well as millions of dollars. It is must reading for anyone with an aging parent."

Terry Savage
***Terry Savage Talks Money,* WBBM–TV (CBS)**
Chicago Sun Times

"The best book on the subject."

Ken and Daria Dolan, authors and radio/TV hosts
***Smart Money,* CNBC; Talknet; WOR–AM, New York**

"This compassionate attorney explains how, by understanding the law, people can save a significant amount of their assets, including their homes."

Golden Years Magazine

"A superb job of creating order out of chaos."

Massachusetts Lawyers' Weekly

"Easy to read ... explains clearly some of Medicaid's most complex inscrutabilities."

Library Journal

"Simply written and well–designed ... to help make Medicaid planning options approachable by the nonprofessional reader."

United Retirement Bulletin

"Stripped of the frills, the message [is] pretty simple: If you plan, you and your family can hold on to your money; if you don't, it could all go to pay for a nursing home."

The Boston Globe

"*How to Protect Your Life Savings* gives us, in simple and accessible terms, most of the information we need about a subject we would rather not deal with — but almost surely will have to."

Doris Dawson
former Chair of the Board of National Gray Panthers

How to Protect Your Life Savings From Catastrophic Illness

How to PROTECT Your Life Savings from Catastrophic Illness

HARLEY GORDON
Attorney at Law

Includes a buyer's guide to long–term care insurance

BOSTON

Fourth Edition
Third Edition, second printing published 1996
Third Edition published 1994
Second Edition published 1991
First Edition published 1990

Design:
Nocturne Design/Boris Levitin

Printed in the United States of America
ISBN 0-9642896-0-1
Library of Congress Catalog Card Number: 94-61273

Financial Strategies Press, Inc.
15 Broad Street, #700
Boston, MA 02109

ACKNOWLEDGEMENTS

The author is indebted to Michael and Myra Gilfix, Tim Nay, Vincent J. Russo and Theresa, Mark Woolpert, Harry Margolis, Alex Bove, Jr., and Peter Strauss, friend and mentor whose knowledge, guidance and support were essential in producing this book. They are simply the best!

Thanks to attorney William Friedler, estate and tax planner *extraordinaire.* To Joseph Pulitano for his time and effort in helping explain long–term care insurance and providing information that allows the reader to make intelligent choices. Thanks also to Sheila Sennett Allen for sharing her knowledge.

To my parents, Lewis and Eleanor.

To Emily, Lily and Ben—don't start looking for a nursing home for your old man yet!

To my wife Susan in memory of Ted, Eunice and Big.

To Ken and Daria Dolan deepest thanks and respect. The success of this book is due in no small part to your belief in its author.

And finally, too often one forgets on whose shoulders one stands to reach goals in life; they are the real heroes, and more often than not they are teachers, not those who hit a ball or score a touchdown:

Fred Koss and Vito Sammarco, too soon departed; teachers who knew that a child can accomplish anything in the world. This book is dedicated to your memories.

"A teacher affects eternity; he can never tell where his influence stops." —*Henry Adams*

AUTHOR'S NOTE

What will this book give you?

Knowledge.
Knowledge equals power.
And power equals CONTROL.

We all struggle to keep control over our lives and our assets. Knowledge is the key to control. We learn how to invest, how to save and when to change course. We struggle to maintain our balance.

If you are facing a catastrophic illness, you are beginning to realize what a loss of control can do to your life. Loss of control over your assets is usually not far behind. Lack of knowledge about how to protect life savings exposes you to financial ruin.

Most self–help books encourage you to do–it–yourself. Simply put, it's not a good idea. My assumption is that you *will* need professional help. After reading this book, you will have identified the difficult points which an attorney can help resolve. The wide margins are for you to make notes. Mark this book and take it with you when you see a lawyer.

It is not the intention of this book to encourage you to hide all your assets and claim poverty. You have a responsibility to pay your fair share. It is my intent to help you avoid going bankrupt paying for an illness you have no control over and that already has devastated your family both emotionally and physically.

In lecturing to audiences of professional and senior citizens' groups, I have seen that they have one thing in common—everyone's confused. This manual is written to clear up the confusion. It tells you in simple language not just what the problem is but what you can do about it. It explains the laws, but there isn't a word of "legalese" on these pages.

You may notice that there is some repetition of certain points. That's intentional. Many people go right to the chapter that pertains to their situation, without reading all the background information. We give it to them again so they won't miss anything.

The solutions offered here are not textbook answers. Instead, I have drawn upon my experiences and those of other professionals whom I trust to give you a streetwise understanding of a complex and sometimes bizarre system.

This is the fourth edition. Since this book first came out, readers and audiences have raised other points they'd like to know more about. This expanded edition includes responses to those questions.

After reading this book, you can make your decisions, however painful and difficult they may be, with confidence that you are acting in an informed and responsible manner.

Harley Gordon

TABLE OF CONTENTS

FOREWORD

Whose problem is this?

We are hearing a lot about nursing homes and their cost these days. We hear that nursing homes are expensive. We hear that old people are going into nursing homes and the the taxpayers have to pick up the cost. With the current squeeze on state and federal budgets, people are getting upset at what appears to be yet another drain on the taxpayers' dollars.

What's really happening?

The answer is that we are facing a period of tremendous social change. As we near the end of the century, a national crisis is being played out in the homes of average families all across America. You are contributing to the crisis if you watch your cholesterol, exercise, take your vitamins, and see your doctor regularly, because you are probably going to live longer. In fact, more and more people are living longer. In the next 40 years, the population of people over 65 will almost double. Today, the fastest–growing segment of the population is people 85 and older.

That's what's causing the crisis. With increasing age comes more frailty and illness. On an individual level, families all over the country are coming face to face with sweeping social change as they struggle to take care of the aging members of their families.

When their elders fall victim to a catastrophic illness like a stroke or Alzheimer's disease, families try to take care of them as best and as long as they can. To do it, family members often give up their normal way of life and their peace of mind. Marriages are stressed to the breaking point; children live with constant tension. Taking care of a chronically ill person at home makes the whole family chronically ill.

The idea that selfish people are dumping their relatives in nursing homes is pure myth. In fact, 85 percent of the frail elderly are cared for at home. Of the remaining 15 percent, half have no immediate family and the rest usually have relatives who are themselves frail and elderly.

The problem of coping with a serious illness can be so painful the people who haven't experienced it can hardly imagine it. Every year, countless families struggle against heartbreak and exhaustion and finally give up. In the end, they make what many call the most painful decision of their lives: they put a beloved spouse or parent in a nursing home.

But the heartache doesn't end there. Medicare and private insurance do not cover the cost of long–term care. When one spouse is admitted to a nursing home, in only a few weeks or months, on average, the couple's entire life savings are wiped out.

Then, when their savings are gone, Medicaid, a program for poor people who have no other means to pay, steps in to pick up on the nursing home cost. The state determines how much money the well spouse is allowed to keep. For people of modest means, the at–home spouse may become impoverished and live out the remainder of his or her life perilously close to, or below, the poverty line.

For both spouses, the sick and the healthy, control over their money is gone, and with it goes the dignity, security and independence they worked all their lives to attain. It's terrifying. As one of my elderly clients put it, "I wake up every morning in fear."

This does not have to happen. In fact, social policy recognizes that impoverishment is wrong. Therefore, the law allows us to avoid financial ruin. There are a number of strategies to do this, but there is always a downside.

When assets are protected, Medicaid, a form of welfare, is all that's left to pick up the cost.

And that makes many taxpayers furious. Their argument goes, "I don't want my tax dollars to pay for your mother's nursing home bill." In short, "It's your problem; you handle it."

Given the seriousness of the threat, people need to have a way to protect themselves. Unfortunately, there are few alternatives that responsible people can utilize.

Long–term care insurance is one answer we will explore. Although earlier policies had restrictions, exceptions, and fuzzy language that may have disqualified the policy–holder from ever collecting much of anything, recent policies have improved substantially and can provide needed coverage. In addition, the recent passage of the Health Insurance Portability Act, also referred to as the Kennedy–Kassebaum bill, offers substantial tax incentives for purchasing long–term care insurance.

In the meantime, what some people are doing is protecting themselves as best they can by using the provisions available under the law. Are these people "flimflamming Medicaid" by taking advantage of loopholes to dump their relatives onto the taxpayers' backs? Are they welfare freeloaders, "false poor" riding a "gravy train," as one national magazine asserts?

Here's a typical story:

My father died from a hereditary disorder that caused a long, slow degeneration of his mind and body. I helped my mother care for him until he mercifully suffered a fatal stroke. I'm convinced that the enormous effort contributed to my mother's death a year after his.

Now I am at risk of the disease. I am 16 years older than my wife. I have two children and a disabled brother who depends upon us for assistance, financial and otherwise.

My wife inherited a house from her mother. We both work full–time and try to save money for our old age. With two children and my brother, it isn't easy to put money aside. I worry constantly about how my family will manage if I develop the disease. I have to do everything I can, now, to protect them if something happens to me.

This case is the norm, not the exception. Sure, there are probably a few wealthy people with high–priced lawyers and accountants who are getting their relatives on Medicaid. True, Medicaid was designed to provide for the poor who have no other means to pay for long–term care. But that's the point — there is no system for the middle class. Does that mean that it makes sense to drive millions of elderly Americans into poverty before we lend them a hand?

Most people accept responsibility for dealing with misfortunes that befall them, even those that occur through no fault of their own. Most people are willing to pay their fair share.

But what is a fair share? What does society owe to the millions of hard–working senior citizens whose taxes have carried this country's economy for half a century? There is no blame or culpability here. Catastrophic illness is an act of God. People do not choose to become critically ill.

When they have outlived their good health and independence, should society say, "Hey, it's your problem; you handle it"?

This issue is a one of the biggest challenges we face as we move toward the next century. It is an individual problem; it is a social problem: Where does responsibility lie? We are being called upon to examine our fundamental beliefs about ourselves and our society.

We operate on the basic assumption that it is the individual's responsibility to society to work for the greatest good for the greatest number. That's why we obey the laws and pay our taxes.

Conversely, it is society's responsibility to the individual to do the same. The whole, in its magnitude, promotes the well–being of the individual. That's why, when an earthquake, hurricane or other act of God strikes, our collective taxes and insurance reserves pay for disaster relief. But when catastrophic illness strikes, there is no adequate "disaster relief."

Senior citizens have held up their end of the bargain. We as a society are not holding up ours.

The problem, in the proportions we are witnessing today, is new. Government and private industry have not yet come up with the answers. Until they do, individuals must use whatever legal means are available to protect themselves.

It's legal, but is it right?

Let's get one thing straight: There is nothing, NOTHING, that middle–class seniors detest more than the idea of being on Medicaid. Call it what you will, this system has the shame and stigma of welfare all over it.

For people who have prided themselves on a lifetime of independence and self–sufficiency, taking Medicaid is accepting defeat. The reason they do it is because they usually have to, sooner or later.

A vulnerable existence, the elderly's daily lives are made easier or more difficult by the machinations of huge social systems that protect some of them and allow others to fall through the cracks.

Today, there are a couple of systems that are working quite well for the elderly. One, Social Security, is an entitlement program that guarantees income after retirement. The word "entitlement" means that everybody who has held a job and paid Social Security taxes is entitled to benefits, generally in rough proportion to their contributions. For many, this program alone has provided whatever financial security they have in their old age.

Another system, Medicare, is also an entitlement program that benefits the elderly. Those who have paid into the system receive assistance with medical bills. For all its awkward paperwork and incomplete coverage, older people are grateful for the protection, albeit incomplete, that Medicare provides.

Since the benefits of both these programs are available to the vast majority of the elderly, regardless of whether their present financial status is sound or shaky, neither stigmatizes the receivers of the systems' largesse. "Assisting all, they humiliate none," according to Richard Margolis in his book, *Risking Old Age in America.*

Not so Medicaid. Medicaid is a means–tested assistance program, with about 70 percent of its disbursements going to the elderly. "Means–tested" means one must *qualify* to receive assistance. In order to qualify, one must be abjectly poor.

This is how Margolis describes Medicaid:

> ...whereas it is mainly Medicare that serves the middle–class elderly in their pursuit of affordable health care, it is chiefly Medicaid that abets their financial struggles in nursing homes. But by that time they are no longer

> middle–class — they are destitute. For a salient feature of Medicaid is that it does nothing to dispel poverty; it manufactures it...
>
> Medicaid is a crucible for downward mobility, compelling families to "spend down" their assets before the government will consent to prop them up. "Spend down" is a government euphemism for parting with one's social security and life savings, and in most cases the process is not lengthy.

According to a recent study by the House Select Committee on aging, within one year, over 90 percent of elderly nursing home residents had depleted their assets and incomes and were impoverished. For two–thirds of single people, the loss occurs in a matter of weeks.

The same study also concluded that 40% of all people over 65 make less than $10,000 a year. This is the class of invisible elderly poor. Over a third more make between $10,000 and $30,000. These people live in daily fear for their financial security. A serious illness or the death of a spouse can tip them suddenly into poverty.

Nor is the next rung on the financial ladder well secured. Even for this relatively affluent group with income between $30,000 and $50,000 a year, a long–term illness can mean catastrophe. With nursing homes costing about that much annually, impoverishment even of this group can occur with stunning speed.

What we see here is that virtually the entire senior population is financially vulnerable. Juxtapose that picture against this one: In the 65–plus age group, almost half will spend time in a nursing home, most between a year and five years or more.

The collision of these two forces, widespread financial vulnerability and massive long–term care needs, will create destitution for millions at a time in their lives when their capacity to recover is at its lowest ebb. As each falls into the problem, he or she may drag other family members, spouses and dependents, closer to the brink of poverty.

Middle class people worry about using Medicaid to protect themselves from financial devastation. They may know it's legal, but they feel it isn't "right." Medicaid is, after all, welfare. The stigma associated with welfare adds insult to injury. But for many, the alternative to using Medicaid now is the likelihood of needing it just a little farther down the line.

As a society we must develop a more humane program, guaranteeing to all protection from the financial ravages of long–term illness. By raising the threshold, we can allow people to qualify for assistance with more dignity. In the words of Richard Margolis:

> We must look at ways to take the sting out of Medicaid assistance. When the price of rescue is pauperization, the rescue itself becomes compromised. The practice of compulsory "spending down" is a throwback to the days of alms houses and public auctions. It makes no sense in a civilized modern society, much less in the world's richest nation.

The problem

At the turn of the century, the average life expectancy in the United States was 47 years. As we reach the last decade of this century, life expectancy has increased to nearly 80 years and people commonly live much longer. By the year 2030, the 65–plus population will more than double; one in every five Americans will be 65 or older.

The longer we live, the more we become susceptible to frailties and illnesses that may incapacitate rather than kill us. As a society and as individuals we are facing some fundamental questions in our struggle to care for an expanding older population.

One of the major problems is: Who takes care of us when we can't manage on our own anymore? Who takes care of our parents? Who takes care of people who are so incapacitated that they need long–term custodial attention?

More and more, the answer is a nursing home. Nursing homes provide long–term custodial care for conditions or illnesses that incapacitate a person—Alzheimer's and related senile dementia, Parkinson's disease, crippling rheumatoid arthritis, stroke, and other major disabilities.

According to a recent study published in *The New England Journal of Medicine*, of people who turned 65 in 1990, 43 percent will enter a nursing home at some time before they die. More than half of those people will spend at least a year there, and almost a quarter will spend at least five years of their lives there. Those are sobering statistics.

The costs are just as disturbing. In the Northeast, the cost of a nursing home bed can easily run up to $75,000 a year. Although the cost may be less in other parts of the country, income and savings are proportionately less as well. Few people can afford those kinds of expenses.

Ultimately the question arises: Who pays for long–term nursing home care? As we will see, there are few sources available.

People work and struggle a lifetime to set aside enough to provide security for themselves and their offspring. The first step in dealing with the problem of protecting assets from chronic illness and long–term nursing home care is to learn about it. Knowledge is the best preparation for confronting the problem head on.

We will look at ways to protect assets in two scenarios:

First: When there is time to plan because the illness has been diagnosed early and progresses slowly.

Second: When there is a crisis, such as a stroke or an accident that requires long–term care immediately.

CHAPTER 1

ALTERNATIVES TO NURSING HOMES

Continuing care retirement communities

In the past several years, there has been a nationwide proliferation of retirement communities. Developers who want to cash in on the burgeoning population of elderly people are aggressively marketing this relatively new product. Many of these facilities promise to care for you for the rest of your life, even if your health fails and you become incapacitated.

Without discussing her plans with anyone, Mrs. Berman, a widow, signed an agreement with a retirement community and paid a fee of more than $60,000. Less than two years later, when her health declined, she received notice that she had to leave within 30 days. The reason they gave was, "your physical and mental condition fails to meet the standards set by the Corporation." Now, more than a year later, they are still holding her money, plus a "service fee" of $600 and a "room preparation fee" of $5,900 for cleaning up her spotless apartment after she left.

Mrs. Berman's dream has turned into a nightmare that many older Americans are experiencing. She was enticed by the promised security of a "life care" or "continuing care retirement community" (CCRC).

In theory, the idea of continuing care is terrific. The tenant signs a contract and pays an "entrance fee" which buys a life–time residency in the facility. A monthly fee provides for services such as meals, housekeeping, laundry and nursing care, if needed.

Unfortunately, these agreements can be a minefield of problems. According to the contract Mrs. Berman signed, the facility does indeed have the right to terminate the contract on the basis of her health, and put her out within 30 days.

To add insult to injury, upon cancellation the facility may keep a substantial portion of her money as determined by a complicated formula spelled out in her contract. Another blow: they don't have to refund any of her money until her unit has been "resold" to a new occupant. The service fee and room preparation charge? They're legal too — it's all in the contract!

A warning to all those considering entering a Continuing Care Retirement Community: An agreement with a CCRC is a binding legal contract involving your security and a lot of your hard–earned money. Have it reviewed by your lawyer or financial advisor. You both might profit from reading the ABA Checklist for Analyzing CCRC Contracts available from the Commission on Legal Problems of the Elderly, 1800 M Street, N.W., Washington, D.C. 20036.

If you are considering a CCRC, check to see if it is accredited by

Continuing Care Accreditation Commission
1129 20th Street NW, Suite 400
Washington, DC 20036
(202) 828-9439

or the industry's self–regulatory body,

The American Association of
Homes for the Aging (AAHA)
1050 17th Street
Washington, DC 20036.

Assisted living

Since the last edition, assisted living facilities have become more of a player in the field of long–term care. In many ways they are similar to CCRC's, but generally are rental units. They provide increasing levels of care as the resident grows more frail. Their popularity has increased because nursing home owners are looking for ways to hedge their bets against Medicaid. As you will see, Medicaid pays much less for a patient than if he were to pay out of his own funds. This, combined with Medicaid's continuing efforts to scale back funding, has convinced the industry to seek out private payers earlier in the aging process. Medicaid will not pay for assisted living. Monthly costs vary widely depending on the level of services available and location. In the midwest, figure $1,800 to $2,500 per month. In the northeast it's usually $3,000. For more information on assisted living, call:

Continuing Care Accreditation Commission
1129 20th Street NW, Suite 400
Washington, DC 20036
(202) 828-9439

Assisted Living Facilities Association
9411 Lee Highway
Fairfax, VA 20031
(703) 691-8100

Where else can you turn?

Contrary to popular belief, nursing homes are not places that families choose as their first option; they are a last resort. Families will struggle for years to keep their parents or relatives out of a nursing home.

With few exceptions, such as a stroke or an accident, most conditions that incapacitate people start slowly and run their downhill course over a period of years. At the beginning, it is easy for a family to overlook the financial impact of providing care at some future date when the sick person's health has deteriorated. Family members tend to hope that they will somehow be able to manage at home.

Unfortunately, best intentions notwithstanding, people underestimate the physical, emotional, and logistical burdens created by trying to cope with a person who is seriously ill. If they do recognize these problems, the family often assumes that a hospital will be a resource when the time comes that they cannot handle the burdens.

That is no longer the case. Here's why:

Hospitals — not anymore!

Hospitals have historically been paid through one of four sources:

- Cash
- Medicare
- Medicaid
- Private insurance (such as HMOs and Blue Cross/Blue Shield)

Cash A hospital stay in most metropolitan areas can cost up to $1,000 or more a day depending upon type of care.

Medicare Medicare should not be confused with Medicaid. Medicare is the primary insurance plan that covers people on social security. It pays for hospital and medical expenses. The vast majority of older people in hospitals are covered by Medicare.

Prior to 1984, Medicare paid whatever bills were submitted by the hospital for a person's care. The expense to the federal government was so enormous that in 1984 the system was drastically reformed. The federal government established a reimbursement system called Diagnosis Related Groupings (DRGs). Under this system, Medicare pays the hospital a flat rate for a person's illness. If the hospital can stabilize the patient for a cost that is less than what Medicare pays, they keep the change. On the other hand, if the patient cannot be stabilized for the designated amount, the hospital usually pays the additional costs out–of–pocket. Therefore, there is a strong economic incentive for a hospital to move a patient out as soon as he is stabilized.

As a result the word "stabilized" has a much different meaning today than it did prior to 1984. In the old days, a person could stay in the hospital almost indefinitely, until he either got significantly better or died. Today, stabilized does not mean that the patient has gotten better at all. It means that the hospital has determined that the illness won't get any worse.

A man was shocked at the treatment his mother received from a hospital. His mother had suffered a stroke and it was apparent to her son that she was still gravely ill. He felt that the hospital should keep her until she was "stabilized" and ready to go home. The hospital said she had to go. It was the hospital's opinion that she would not have another stroke and by their definition, she was "stabilized" and ready to be discharged.

Under the law, the hospital had the right to discharge his mother. She was discharged in a semi–conscious state, on a catheter, and with a feeding tube going into her stomach.

The remaining possible methods of payment are Medicaid, cash, and private insurance.

Medicaid This health care system is funded by both the state and federal government. It is only available to the financially needy. Unlike Medicare, there are no deductibles. It pays when nothing else will.

Private insurance (such as HMOs and Blue Cross/Blue Shield) There are numerous health care plans which people can buy or which are provided by employers to pay for hospital care. Most private insurers now have a form of DRGs that they use to limit costs.

Taking a chronically ill person home

Regardless of who pays for the hospital, one thing is certain—hospitals are no longer places to get better. Once the patient is stabilized, the family must quickly find another place to care for him. At that point, there are usually only two options left: take the sick person home or put him in a nursing home.

When the sick person's illness or disability takes a mild form, home care may be a viable option for a while. But what happens when he cannot feed or clothe himself or take care of bodily functions without assistance? What if he is incontinent, in pain, depressed, unruly, or hostile? What happens when he cannot be left alone during waking hours? When he must be lifted from a bed to a wheelchair to the toilet and back?

What about the daughter who can't leave the house for twenty minutes because her mother might fall or set the house on fire? There is a saying about dealing with chronically ill people at home: Dealing with someone who is chronically ill eventually makes healthy people chronically ill. The care giver becomes a virtual prisoner in the house. The world closes down. Life as it was before the illness is gone completely.

And who is the care giver? The burdens of caring for our aging population fall disproportionately on women. It is usually the wife, daughter or daughter–in–law who sacrifices her way of life to take care of the chronically ill family member. Often she has sole responsibility in this difficult task. Her life takes a back seat to the needs of the sick person who requires care twenty–four hours a day. She may quit a job and give up all her other activities outside the home. The stress on her is enormous.

The situation affects members of the family not directly responsible for giving care. Families have been known to fall apart over taking care of mother or father. Some marriages are driven to the brink of divorce by the tremendous pressure of coping with the problem.

While the ideal of caring for an incapacitated family member at home is what every loving family aspires to, the realities of the situation are often so difficult that no amount of love, sacrifice, or denial can make it work.

What is left is the last viable, though often least desired, alternative: placement in a nursing home.

The nursing home

Nursing homes provide basically three types of care. They are:

- Medically necessary care (which in many ways approximates hospital care) for which Medicare will pay for a period of time.

- Skilled nursing care which provides patients with continuous care and assistance by nurses and other medical professionals.
- Intermediate care for those who need help with everyday routine activities.

Medicare or other types of medical insurance plans will not pay for skilled nursing care or intermediate care since they are considered custodial care. The yearly cost for this kind of care averages $60,000 in the Northeast and West Coast and $40,000 nationally. Many people have the mistaken idea that there exists some system or institution which will pay these bills.

People sometimes assume that the Veterans' Administration will pay for veterans who need custodial care. The VA rarely pays unless care is required because of a service–related illness or injury.

So how do people manage when confronted by an overwhelmingly confusing financial dilemma?

Who pays — How the system works

Few people want to escape reasonable financial responsibility for unfortunate circumstances in their own lives. Most people are more than willing to pay their fair share. But in every situation, there comes a point when enough is enough. The central issue in preserving a family's well–being is the ability to have a measure of control when a catastrophic illness hits.

Make no mistake about it: If families do not take steps early on to protect their assets from the consequences of a long–term illness, they *will* lose control. When that happens, there may be little or nothing left to provide for the surviving spouse and their offspring.

So we go back again to the question: Who pays for long–term nursing home care?

The answer is disturbing.

- Private health insurance companies, such as Blue Cross/Blue Shield, will not pay for custodial care.
- The Veterans' Administration, in most cases, will not pay.
- Health Maintenance Organizations (HMOs) or similar insurance plans will not pay.
- Medicare will not pay.

In fact, there are *only three* sources to pay for long–term nursing home care:

- cash
- Medicaid
- long–term care insurance

Cash At a national average cost of $40,000 a year for nursing home care, studies have shown that the average family's life savings will be wiped out in a matter of weeks or months.

Medicaid No one likes to apply for public assistance. It is one of the great ironies that the very system that older Americans have struggled for years to avoid, for many will be the only means to pay for nursing home care.

Long–term care insurance Insurance companies offer plans that will pay certain amounts towards daily custodial and/or skilled care for a period of years. These policies may be the right answer for those who fear the financial consequences of nursing home confinement but want to maintain control for as long as possible.

If you understand how these systems work, your life savings need not be wiped out. It is possible to protect your savings for a surviving spouse or to take care of your children should they need assistance in the future.

Before you go forward, it is important that you understand the current climate of using Medicaid to pay for long–term care. The intent of Congress was to offer this needs–based program for those who could not afford the cost of a catastrophic illness. By default this ended up including the middle class as well as those less fortunate. While this appeared acceptable, what wasn't was having the program considered a middle–class entitlement.

Medicaid was and is intended for those who are financially strapped as well as those who are too ill to afford other alternatives such as long–term care insurance. Whether rightly or wrongly, Congress now feels the program has been abused by those who think Medicaid is a right. Unfortunately, this has been reinforced by some professionals who look at the program as a first, not a last, option.

The book is intended to help those who have no other options available to pay for this most expensive of care. It is for those who are already ill or have very limited resources. It is for those who have a spouse who herself may go on public benefits if steps are not taken to protect modest funds, or have children who are disabled and may need resources to assist them after their parents are gone.

As you will see, Congress has taken decisive and harsh steps to deal with those who believe Medicaid is a first option and therefore resort to Medicaid planning. The use of trusts, in particular, has come under sustained attack.

Which, by the way, is another reason for this book. It will suggest that those who are considering a Medicaid plan, or have already put one together, may end up paying more in taxes than, say, the premiums on a long–term care insurance policy. And that's assuming the plan is legal in the first place!

It's time to get educated. Let's look at the law and see how the law looks at your assets.

Because the federal government allows each state a certain amount of flexibility in applying the law, the following information by nature must state only general principles. Regulations change constantly. Be sure to call your local Department of Public Welfare to see if the rules have changed.

CHAPTER 2

THE BASICS – UNDERSTANDING MEDICAID

Assets

Under the current system, there are two factors that determine eligibility for public assistance: assets and income.

Assets: Definition — everything you own that has value.

That definition seems simple enough. Medicaid, however, divides assets into three categories. Don't try to make sense out of why a particular asset falls into one category and not another. No one ever said that the Medicaid program was rational. In fact, it sometimes appears that Medicaid is as confused as we are in trying to figure out what they will take and what they will let us keep.

The three groups of assets are: countable, non–countable and inaccessible.

Countable assets

Countable assets (also called non–exempt assets) These are things that Medicaid wants you to spend to zero before financial assistance is available.

They include:

- Cash over $2,000 (in most states)

- Stocks
- Bonds
- IRAs
- Keoghs
- Certificates of deposit
- Single premium deferred annuities
- Treasury notes and treasury bills
- Savings bonds
- Investment property
- Whole life insurance above a certain amount
- Vacation homes
- Second vehicles
- Every other asset that is not specifically listed as non–countable is included in this list.

These are things that are in jeopardy when catastrophic illness strikes. In order to qualify for Medicaid, the applicant must in effect be BANKRUPT.

Non–countable assets

Non–countable assets (also called exempt assets) Believe it or not, these things can be worth hundreds of thousands of dollars but Medicaid has chosen not to count them in determining eligibility. These assets are not in immediate jeopardy.

They include:

- A house used as a primary residence (in most states this includes two– and three–family homes)
- An amount of cash (usually $2,000)
- A car
- Personal jewelry
- Household effects
- A prepaid funeral
- A burial account (not to exceed $2,500 in most states)
- Term life insurance policies (as opposed to whole life) which have no cash surrender value
- Business property (be sure to check in your state, this is a little known exception)

Life insurance is generally divided into two groups: whole life and term. Whole life has a cash value which increases the longer you hold the policy. Although the insurance lapses when you stop paying, you receive cash value back. This is called the policy's surrender value.

Term insurance never builds up a cash value, but pays a set amount when you die. Coverage stops when you stop paying. Most states allow you to keep unlimited term insurance when applying for Medicaid but only a limited amount of whole life insurance. The maximum face value most states allow is $1,500. You therefore end up losing the death benefit which may be of much greater value than the cash surrender value which would have to be spent on your nursing home costs.

Inaccessible assets

Inaccessible assets – These are countable assets which have been made unavailable to Medicaid. To put it bluntly, *if you can't get them, they can't get them.*

Assets are made inaccessible by

1. Giving them away
2. Holding them in trusts (see below)

Medicaid trusts

Holding assets in Medicaid trusts There are two kinds of trusts to consider: revocable and irrevocable. The difference between the two is the first you can change after it is set up, the second, you can't. Regardless of what type of trust you have, the purpose is the same, to hold assets.

In a **revocable trust** (also called a living trust), there must be at least one trustee and one or more beneficiaries. A trustee is simply the person who makes the decisions for the trust. The beneficiary is the person who gets the benefit of the assets in the trust. Since you make the trust, you make the rules that the trustee must follow. If you don't like the trust, you can change it or do away with it. That's why it is called revocable.

A revocable trust also acts as a will. The rules you make can include who gets your money and under what conditions after you die. While you are alive you receive the benefits. This kind of trust has not been useful in protecting countable assets because Medicaid simply assumes that if you control the assets, they are available to be spent in your care. That continues to be the case.

However, at one time a revocable trust was effective in protecting your home because the state could only place a lien on it if it was in your probated estate. Since an asset owned by a trust does not go through your estate, there would be no lien. That was then, but the rules have changed.

Every state now "sees through" revocable trusts. If your home is currently in one, most likely you will be unable to qualify for Medicaid even if you have no assets. You will be required to re–transfer your house to your name in order to qualify. Your state will then place a lien on the property for recovery of benefits paid on your behalf.

Under no circumstances can you transfer your home to your children directly from a trust. As of August 11, 1993, the transfer will create a "look–back" period of 5 years. Depending on the value of your home, failure to understand the ineligibility period could cost you the entire value of your house. For a complete explanation of the "look–back" and ineligibility rules, please see Chapter 3.

An **irrevocable trust**, like a revocable trust, is a legal instrument that you set up to hold assets. Like a revocable trust, there must be one or more trustees and one or more beneficiaries. The definition of a trustee and beneficiary are the same as above. You can make the same rules. The difference is that once you've made the rules you can't change them. By making it irrevocable you give up the power to modify or do away with the trust. Simply put, you give up control.

A brief history of irrevocable trusts in Medicaid planning

The beginning of time to 1986

In the past, seniors who understood that they could lose their life savings if they ended up in a nursing home sought the help of elder law attorneys who advised them to set up an irrevocable trust and place their life savings in it. The parents (called the donors) would name themselves as the beneficiaries and appoint one of their children as a trustee. The donors would instruct the trustee to give them income and principal whenever the trustee chose. Of course while the parents were healthy the trustee would give them whatever they wanted.

If one parent got sick the trustee would exercise discretion and give his parents nothing. Since the trust was irrevocable the parents could not order the trustee to give them assets, therefore the parent would qualify for Medicaid.

June 1, 1986 to August 11, 1993

Congress passed a law that took effect on June 1st 1986 restricting the use of irrevocable trusts. It said that if you set up an irrevocable trust, name yourself as a beneficiary, and give power to your trustee to give you all, some or none of the income and assets, Medicaid will assume your trustee will make all the income and principal available to you and thus the nursing home. It doesn't matter that your trustee can say, "I have the power to refuse to give the nursing home any money." Medicaid won't buy it. These instruments were generally referred to as "irrevocable discretionary" trusts. After the law went into effect, they are now called Medicaid Qualifying Trusts or "MQT's".

WARNING: There are thousands of these types of trusts still in existence. Most were drafted before June 1, 1986. The law retroactively banned their use. Believe it or not, there are attorneys who are still drafting them! The safe bet is to take any trusts that you have to a competent attorney and have them checked out.

As a result of the 1986 change, lawyers scrambled to come up with an instrument that would protect assets while giving their clients as much control as possible and access to their assets. Here are a number of variations:

Income–only trusts

Ed and Mary establish the Jones Family Irrevocable Trust. They name themselves as the beneficiaries and their son Peter as the trustee. They place $50,000 in it. The terms are simple: The trustee has no discretion over principal; it stays in the trust and cannot be distributed. Income, however, can be given to Ed and Mary as beneficiaries. Upon the death of the survivor, the principal goes to the children.

Since Peter cannot give principal to his parents, Medicaid is powerless to declare it available to the nursing home. Result: One half of income will go to the nursing home if Ed or Mary need care, but 100 percent of the principal is protected.

"Trigger" trusts

Ed and Mary establish the Jones Family Irrevocable Trust. They name themselves as the beneficiaries and their son, Peter, the trustee. They place $50,000 in it. The terms are not so simple: While either Ed or Mary is healthy, the trustee has full discretion to give either or both income or principal. If Ed or Mary becomes ill (not necessarily placed in a nursing home) the trust states that Peter loses his authority to give principal or interest to his parents. Ed and Mary would be barred from *receiving Medicaid for up to 30 months. However, both would qualify after that period.*

Indirect Irrevocable Trusts

Ed and Mary establish the Jones Family Irrevocable Trust. They name themselves as beneficiaries but of the income only. They cannot be given principal by the trustee, their son Peter. They place $50,000 in it. The terms: Ed and Mary's children, Peter, Thomas and Deborah are beneficiaries also. They can receive principal from Peter at his discretion. Peter could make a distribution to any of his siblings who in turn could gift it to the parents.

Three strikes and you're out? Using income–only and trigger trusts after OBRA '93

First, in order to understand what Congress did under the Omnibus Budget Reconciliation Act of 1993 (OBRA '93, which became effective on August 11, 1993), you must first understand what their intent appeared to be. Congress didn't like income–only trusts. Congress didn't like "trigger trusts". Congress didn't like indirect irrevocable trusts. Congress didn't like any trust that could protect income or assets! What came next, however, has caused a great deal of confusion. There appear to be two schools of thought: First, the law; then, the opinions. Here is the language as it appeared in the statute that has wreaked havoc with Medicaid planning:

"...if there are any circumstances under which payment from the (irrevocable) trust could be made to or for the benefit of the individual (or his or her spouse), the portion of the corpus (principal) from which or the income on the corpus from which payment to the individual (or his or her spouse) could be made shall be considered a resource available to the individual."

Majority opinion: As of 1997, income–only trusts are valid in protecting principal. However, under OBRA '93, Congress allowed the states to enact a so–called estate recovery program. Most professionals believe that the language in the bill allows your state to place a lien on the principal in an income–only trust. Please see the following section, "Estate recovery".

I, for one, have not drafted an income–only trust since 1993.

The use of trigger trusts has also been severely restricted. Many states have declared that they are against public policy. Please be very careful in using any trust, or relying upon a preexisting trust, if the intent is to protect assets from catastrophic illness.

If you do use a trust, please remember: the "look–back" period for making transfers into or out of certain types of trusts has been raised to 5 years. For a detailed explanation, please see Chapter 3.

Estate recovery

Medicaid provisions of the Omnibus Budget Reconciliation Act of 1993 (OBRA '93) mandate recovery programs from a recipient's estate. An estate has traditionally been defined as any assets that are left in a person's name alone, or benefits or proceeds from investments that would be made payable to his estate upon his death.

The new law is vague as to what Medicaid may consider to be part of your estate. For example, it states an estate may include such "...assets conveyed to a survivor, heir, or assign of the deceased individual through joint tenancy, tenancy in common, survivorship, life estate, living trust, or other arrangements."

A traditional interpretation of "estates" would not include assets held in joint tenancy, since the surviving owner gets the deceased partner's share automatically.

This law now casts doubt on the use of income–only trusts and life estates, because assets held in this form of ownership are brought back into your taxable estate when you die.

The long and short of the matter is that you should be very careful in keeping an interest in assets even though you may not own or control them, because even though they may not be in your estate when you die, Medicaid could claim the entire value of the asset because you had an interest in it.

The spousal allowance

In 1988, Congress passed regulations that were intended to protect the spouse not in a nursing home (referred to as the community spouse). In 1997, the at–home spouse is allowed to keep a certain amount of countable assets, called the Community Spousal Resource Allowance (CSRA), by using the following formula:

Step 1 — Medicaid fixes the day a spouse goes into a nursing home or medical institution.

Step 2 — Medicaid requires that the couple list all their countable assets regardless of whose name they are in, who earned them or how long they've been in either's name, including any assets that were transferred within the past 36 months (60 months if transferred into certain types of trust, see Chapter 3).

Step 3 — Medicaid takes a "snapshot," a picture of the combined assets on the day the spouse goes into the nursing home or a hospital for 30 days or more.

Step 4 — The stay–at–home spouse (technically referred to as the "community spouse") is then allowed to keep one–half of the total amount of the assets in the snapshot, but not less than $15,804 ("floor")or more than $79,020 ("ceiling"), as of this writing (1997). This figure will be raised annually.

Example: Curtis is going into a nursing home on June 1st, 1997. He and his wife Helen have total assets of $20,000; $15,000 of which is in his IRA. Medicaid will take a snapshot of the couple's combined assets on June 1st. Helen will be allowed to keep one–half of $20,000. But since one–half of $20,000 is $10,000, less than the minimum, she will be allowed to keep $15,804, the floor.

If Curtis and Helen had $150,000, Helen would be allowed to keep half, $75,000, not the ceiling of $79,020.

To make matters a little more confusing, although the principles here are consistent across the board, the dollar amounts may vary from state to state. The law allows each state to raise the floor of $15,804 all the way to the ceiling of $79,020. Here's how that works:

Your state may decide to raise the "floor" on the amount an at–home spouse may keep of the couple's joint assets. Rather than a floor of $15,804, they raise it to $40,000. What happens in our example when the floor is raised to $40,000? Helen would be allowed to keep the entire $20,000 because her state raised the floor from $15,804 to $40,000 (see Questionnaire 1, Chapter 12, to determine what floor your state has set).

If assets must be spent down by the institutionalized spouse in order to qualify, the application for Medicaid may not take place for months. Regardless of what the total assets are on the day he applies, the at–home spouse's share will always be determined on the day of the snapshot.

Example: Joel and Esther have combined countable assets of $100,000 when Esther goes into a nursing home on January 1. The snapshot is taken on that day. Joel's spousal share in his state (the amount he is allowed to keep) is $50,000. Unless Esther buys non–countable assets or otherwise protects her money, she will have to spend $48,000 on her care ($50,000 minus the $2,000 cash allowance their state allows).

Let's say that Esther applies for Medicaid a year after paying privately for the nursing home. There is now $70,000 left of countable assets. All Esther would have to spend is an additional $18,000. Why? Because Medicaid goes back to January 1 to determine Joel's share ($50,000). This amount deducted from $70,000 leaves $20,000 that is Esther's share to pay the nursing home. She is allowed to keep $2,000 of that amount.

You may be confused in thinking that in taking the snapshot, you are applying for Medicaid. That's not the case unless the snapshot reveals that your assets are less than the maximum limit to qualify for Medicaid. If the assets exceed these amounts, you must then spend down to the limits set by your state.

Income

Definition — Income is all money you receive from any source. Like countable assets, it is in jeopardy.

The money may come from one or a combination of the following:

- Social security
- Interest and investments
- Trusts
- Rental units
- Help from family members
- Pensions
- Annuities

Income eligibility is quite simple. In all states, if the person going into the nursing home has monthly income that exceeds the nursing home bill, he pays the nursing home directly.

In about half the states, if the patient's monthly income is less than the nursing home bill, just about all of it goes to the home and Medicaid makes up the difference based upon what it pays the nursing home.

The remainder set a "cap" on your monthly income. As of this writing (1997), it is $1,452 per month. If the applicant's monthly income exceeds this amount, he or she cannot qualify for Medicaid unless he or she sets up a "Miller" trust (Chapter 5).

Income for the community spouse

Most states allow a person to keep:

- a personal needs allowance (approximately $40, depending on the state)
- a home maintenance allowance if planning to go home
- a monthly premium to pay for medical insurance

Income rules do not apply to the at–home spouse. He or she is free to continue working and keep all salary and other monthly income such as social security. In addition, the state usually allows the at–home spouse to keep half of assets that generate income, such as dividends, rent, etc.

Federal law requires states to set a specified amount the at–home spouse may keep from total joint income. As of this writing (1997), the minimum is $1,326.25 per month, the maximum $1,975.50. The states have discretion in setting the amount within those limits. The at–home spouse has the opportunity to increase the state–set amount if she can show that her housing expenses are unusually high.

The Resource–First Rule

In 1993, Congress passed legislation that allows the community spouse to keep more of the institutionalized spouse's asset spend–down to generate the monthly income to bring the spouse at home up to $1,326.25 (this is the floor, the spouse could receive up to $1,975.50 if she could prove need). Here's how it works:

Dennis' and Eleanor's only income is $2,000 a month in Social Security benefits. Of that, $1,500 is the husband's, $500 is his wife's. The couple has assets of $279,020.

If Dennis goes into a nursing home, Eleanor will be allowed to keep a monthly minimum needs allowance of, in her state, $1,326.25. Since her income is only $500, she will be short $826.25. Here is what will happen:

1. *The state will factor a return on her spousal allowance of $79,020. Each state may set a different rate, but it usually follows the one paid*

on short–term certificates of deposits. Let's say it's 4%. The yearly income is $3,161 or about $263 per month.

2. *Eleanor's monthly income will now be $763. She will still be short $563.25 per month. Under the Resource-First Rule, she may keep whatever amount of her husbands asset spend–down of $200,000 she needs to generate $563.25 per month. If the state sets the interest rate at 4%, Eleanor will be able to keep approximately $169,000 of Dennis's spend-down. Eleanor will also be able to keep her spousal share, $79,020. The remaining $31,000 of Dennis's spend–down, less deductions for things such as a prepaid funeral and small cash allowance, will have to be spent on his care.*

Please remember, your state sets the rate of return and this varies widely.

HOW TO PROTECT ASSETS WHEN THERE IS TIME TO PLAN

As mentioned in Chapter 1, Medicaid is not a middle–class entitlement. It should be used only for those who have medical conditions that preclude more traditional methods of protecting life savings, or do not have sufficient income to purchase long–term care insurance.

When a diagnosis is made early and the illness is expected to progress slowly, the family has time to plan. This is the time to start protecting assets.

The key to protection is knowing what assets and income are in jeopardy and what the critical deadlines are for transferring them. In the preceding Chapter, we identified which assets and income are in jeopardy.

Our goal is to take countable assets (those that have to be spent to zero), and make them either non–countable or inaccessible. In the following chapter, we will look at the options available to people in different situations.

Remember: The key to protecting assets when you have time to plan is understanding the rules about disqualification.

The look–back period

Medicaid has the right to **look back** at your finances for a period of months from the date you first apply for assistance. As of 1997, that period was 3 years. In other words, Medicaid will say to you on the date you apply, "Please supply us with all your financial records for the past 3 years." What they are looking for are withdrawals and deposits of, typically, $1,000 or more.

One other thing to be aware of: As of August 11, 1993 transfers into or out of certain types of trusts will create a 5-year look–back period. What confuses the heck out of most people is that they think the look–back period is the number of months you are disqualified from receiving Medicaid. This is not the case. Read on.

The ineligibility period

Read the following rule several times to be sure you understand it:

If you transfer countable assets for less than fair market value within the look–back period (3 years for outright transfers to another person and 60 months for transfers to or from certain types of trusts), it is presumed that the transfer was made to get assets out of your name in order to qualify for Medicaid. Medicaid, therefore, can declare you ineligible for assistance. You will remain ineligible for a period of time.

The actual period of ineligibility is determined by a formula which depends on two factors: 1) the value of assets you transferred to another person, and, 2) the average monthly nursing home bill in your state.

Here is the formula: The value of assets transferred divided by the average monthly nursing home bill as established by your state's welfare department equals the number of months you are disqualified from receiving Medicaid.

What Medicaid is saying is that if you transferred money to avoid paying for a nursing home, why should they pay? They determine the ineligibility created by the transfer by setting a daily or monthly average cost, then dividing it into the money you transferred. For example, if your state has established $4,500 per month as the average nursing home bill and you transferred $9,000, your ineligibility would be two months. The period of ineligibility begins not when you apply for assistance, but when you transfer the money.

For example, if you transfer $9,000 on January 1, 1997 and can stay out of a nursing home until March 1, 1997, you would thereafter qualify for Medicaid even though the transfer took place within 3 years, because the ineligibility period of two ($9,000 divided by $4500) months has run.

Here are a few more examples to help you understand the concept:

Example: Sam knows he has Parkinson's disease and wants to leave something to his son when he dies. He would like to transfer his assets to his son now, but he is worried that he will need nursing home care within the 36–month ineligibility period and be unable to qualify for assistance. He lives in Massachusetts, which has established $4500 as its monthly average nursing home bill. Here's what happens:

1. *Sam transfers $45,0000 to his son on January 1, 1997.*
2. *He is disqualified from receiving Medicaid for 10 months ($45,000 divided by $4,500).*
3. *Sam applies for Medicaid on December 30, 1998, 24 months after he transferred his assets.*

4. *Medicaid demands to see Sam's bank statements going back 3 years from the day he applied for assistance.*
5. *Sam is not disqualified for another 12 months (a total of 36) because his ineligibility period (10 months as determined by the formula) has already run at the time he applied for Medicaid. In other words, even though Sam applied for Medicaid within the 36 month look–back period, he still qualifies for Medicaid.*

Note that the above rule has come under attack. On January 1, 1997, the Health Insurance Portability Act, also known as the Kennedy–Kassebaum bill, went into effect. One section of that law appears to have effectively criminalized Medicaid planning. Contained in section 217, the provision is titled: "Criminal penalties for acts involving Medicare or State health care programs (Medicaid)." It states:

"Whoever...knowingly and willfully disposes of assets (including by any transfer in trust) in order for an individual to become eligible for medical assistance (Medicaid) under a State plan under title XIX, if disposing of the assets results in the imposition of a period of ineligibility for such assistance shall...be punishable by a fine of up to $10,000 and or up to one year in jail." In

addition your state could disqualify you from Medicaid benefits for up to one year.

There are, as of this writing, two interpretations:

1. If you make any transfer within the look-back period, which is 3 years for outright transfers, and 60 months for transfers into a trust, you have violated the law.
2. The less restrictive interpretation is that if you wait for the ineligibility period to expire (as in the above example), no law has been violated.

The truth of the matter, however, is that no–one has any idea of how this statute will be interpreted. Furthermore, at the time this book went to press, a bill had been introduced to repeal the above criminal sanctions. It is essential that you consult with a competent attorney to determine the status of this repeal effort, to help you make decisions.

Now, what happens if Sam has a bit more money?

1. *Sam transfers $180,000 to his son on January 1, 1997.*
2. *The disqualification period, in Massachusetts, is 40 months ($180,000 divided by $4,500).*

3. *Sam makes the mistake of applying for Medicaid on December 30, 1999, one day short of 3 years.*
4. *Sam is declared ineligible for assistance not just for one day but for another 4 months (40 minus 36) because he applied for assistance within the look back period. Medicaid will look at the transfer and apply the formula we just talked about. Had Sam waited until the full 36 month look back period had run, Medicaid could not have applied the formula because they have no right to "look back" more than 3 years.*

The same law applies to a couple. Transfers by the at–home spouse to children or any other person creates the same ineligibility problems.

Under this rule, failure to thoroughly understand the look–back and ineligibility period could prove disastrous for you. If you make large transfers of money and apply for Medicaid at any time within 3 years of the transfer, your actual ineligibility may far exceed 3 years. Please, before you do anything, sit down with an elder law attorney who is thoroughly versed in Medicaid law. Here's a tip to help you determine if the attorney understands the law: Ask for an explanation of the look–back and ineligibility periods. If you sense any hesitation or confusion in the answer, pick yourself up and leave!

At this point we have covered the general principles in protecting assets. Now let's get down to specifics.

Getting down to business

There is no single course of action that best suits every situation. To demonstrate the various options, we will explore several examples. One of these will closely fit your own situation. The examples cover asset protection for:

- Spouses
- Offspring and parents
- Offspring and single parent
- Siblings
- Nieces/nephews and aunts/uncles
- Grandchildren and grandparents
- Unrelated people

In each example, we will consider the pros and cons of all the options available in these particular circumstances. After reviewing the choices, we will determine which option best suits the needs of the people involved.

Remember one thing throughout these examples: There is a considerable downside to Medicaid planning if there are substantial assets. As previously mentioned, Medicaid was intended for those with limited resources and or have pre–existing medical conditions. If you plan on using this program to protect large sums of money, you will quickly find out that, although you may qualify for benefits in the future, you will have paid a price.

Finally, no professional can tell you with absolute certainty that the plan he or she creates for you today will be valid tomorrow.

The previous examples assume that the family has at least 3 years before nursing home confinement. If you are considering establishing a trust, you should keep in mind that most experts interpret the law to mean that transfers into certain types of trusts will create a 5-year look–back period.

Spouses

This example deals with a spouse who may need nursing home care in the future and how his family can help protect the family's assets. The Andrews have a close and trusting relationship with daughter Susan, but not with son Bill.

NAME:	Mr. and Mrs. Andrews
AGE:	husband: 65 wife: 65
ASSETS:	house (jointly held, no mortgage) $150,000 savings (joint) $48,000 (includes wife's inheritance of $10,000)
INSURANCE:	husband has two insurance policies, a whole life policy with a face value of $10,000 and a cash surrender value of $2,000, and a term policy worth $25,000.
INCOME:	from joint savings $4,000/year social security: husband $650/month wife $300/month
HEALTH:	husband: early Alzheimer's wife: good
FAMILY:	two adult children, Bill and Susan

The goal is to take countable assets and move them to the non–countable or inaccessible column, making sure sufficient assets remain to pay for Mr. Andrews' care. Here is how the assets would be categorized at the time of the Alzheimer's diagnosis before steps are taken to protect them:

non–countable	countable	inaccessible
house	joint savings $48,000	none currently
term policy	whole life insurance policy $2,000 cash surrender value	

If assets remain in the countable column, they will have to be spent on nursing home care, subject to the Community Spousal Resource Allowance (CSRA), before the husband qualifies for financial assistance. If the couple transfer the assets to the inaccessible column within 3 years of the husband's applying for Medicaid, it presumes that he is trying to protect the assets and he will be denied assistance based on the formula previously discussed (funds transferred divided by the average monthly nursing home bill established by your welfare department).

Here's what will happen if the assets remain exactly as they appear above:

On the day the husband goes into the nursing home, Medicaid will take a snapshot of the couple's assets regardless of whose name they are in. Since the countable assets were not shifted to other categories, the wife will be allowed to keep only a specified amount. That figure is arrived at by applying a somewhat confusing formula: As of this writing (1997), she may keep no less than $15,804 (the federal floor) OR one half of their combined total assets up to a limit of $79,020 (the federal ceiling), whichever is greater. Because each state can set its own floor or ceiling within the federal limits, what she actually keeps depends on the state she lives in. See Chapter 12 to determine how much that is. For our example, let's assume it's what most states will allow; one half of the assets if they are greater than the floor but less than the ceiling.

Looking at the Andrews' chart, we see that their joint funds, including the cash surrender value of their life insurance policy, are $50,000. Half of that is $25,000. Since $25,000 is greater than $15,804 and less than $79,020 she is allowed to keep $25,000.

Here's what happens if their countable assets are $15,000 instead of $50,000. One half of $15,000 is $7,500. Because $7,500 is less than $15,804, she gets to keep it all since that's the minimum the law allows.

What would have happened if their savings and accountable assets had been $200,000? One half is

$100,000. Because $100,000 is greater than $79,020, she gets to keep only $79,020 since it is the maximum the law allows.

Individual states are allowed by law to raise the amount the at–home spouse may keep (see Chapter 12 to determine what your state allows).

What happens if the state where the Andrews live raises to $40,000 the minimum amount that the at–home spouse could keep? Our chart shows total countable assets of $50,000. One half of $50,000 is $25,000. Because the floor is now $40,000, the wife in our example gets to keep not one half or $25,000, but $40,000 of their $50,000 in joint assets.

Now, let's say that the couple had $150,000 in joint assets. One half is $75,000. Because $75,000 is less than the ceiling of $79,020, she gets to keep the ceiling.

What happens when the husband and wife have time to plan?

Let's look at the various options we might use to protect those assets if the Andrews have time to plan.

Remember: Assets may be protected by

Option 1 Giving them away (typically to offspring)

Option 2 Holding them in trust

Option 3 Consider the Resource-First Rule (see Chapter 2).

After examining each option, we will see which is best suited for this specific situation.

Option 1 Giving away assets to your children

Here's a little wisdom to ponder: Never give your assets to your children unless you are absolutely, positively willing to stake your life on the belief that they will give them back or make them available to you when you ask.

Here's what you want to avoid:

- The children's spending your money because they "thought it was a gift"
- Your son's or daughter's spouse's (whom you never liked in the first place) getting your assets in a divorce
- Your son's or daughter's losing the money in a bad business deal.

- Your son's or daughter's death.
- If assets that have a low cost basis, such as stock, are given away, the children receive that basis. When the asset is sold there will be a large capital gain. However if the stock remains in the your name, there will be a free cost "step–up" to fair market value when you die. Result: No capital gains tax for the children if they sell the stock.
- If assets are in qualified plans such as IRAs, transferring them means the possibility of penalties and steep income tax consequences.
- Loss of financial aid. If assets are given to children, and they have kids who receive financial aid in private school or college, that aid will probably be jeopardized.

A rule of thumb in determining whether your offspring should be the choice to hold and protect your assets: If you have to think more than one half of one second before you answer "yes," forget the whole idea. On the other hand, if you do have a close and trusting relationship with your offspring, you can enlist their help in protecting your assets. Please think carefully, however, about the consequences of giving assets away.

Option 2 Holding assets in trust

The use of a Medicaid Qualifying Trust will not protect assets. The people who establish such an instrument are its beneficiaries and give discretion over the income and principal to the trustee. Please review Chapter 2.

Income–only trusts, discussed below, may work, but read further.

As of August 11, 1993, owing to the passage of new laws contained in the Omnibus Budget Reconciliation Act of 1993 (OBRA '93), the use of any type of trust, once a basic tool for protecting assets from Medicaid, has been severely restricted. Let's look at several examples of trusts, with an opinion at the end of each one as to whether they will work in this example since the law has changed. For a complete explanation, see Chapter 2.

Example 1 An irrevocable "income–only" trust

The Andrews set up the Andrews Family Trust with their children as trustees and themselves as beneficiaries. They do not give the trustees the power to give them assets, only the power to hold assets in trust while they generate income for their parents. Let's assume the applicable ineligibility period has passed (funds transferred into the trust divided by the average monthly nursing home bill; see Chapter 12). The day Mr. Andrews goes into the nursing home is the day the snapshot is taken of their assets. The assets in the trust are not in the snapshot because the trustees cannot make them available to beneficiaries

Opinion:

Before OBRA '93, the principal in this instrument would be protected as long as the ineligibility period had run. One half of the net income, however, would be available to the spouse entering the nursing home.

Under the 1993 law it is likely that income–only trusts will still protect principal. Even if assets are protected, there is still a chance your state may get them after the death of the trust donors through a procedure called estate recovery. See Chapter 2.

Example 2 A "trigger" trust

Mr. and Mrs. Andrews set up a trust with their children as beneficiaries and one of them, Peter, as trustee. The parents can get principal and income from the trust while both of them are healthy. However, should one of them become ill in the future or go into a nursing home, a change is triggered under the terms of the trust: the trustee is then ordered not to give either parent principal or income and instead to make those funds available to the beneficiaries (the three children). The parents would be ineligible for Medicaid based on the amount of money transferred into the trust (funds transferred divided by the average monthly nursing home bill), but not more than 3 years if set up prior to August 11, 1993, or 60 months after that.

Opinion:

Prior to OBRA '93, it was likely that this type of trust would protect assets and income after the ineligibility period ran. It would begin on the day of entry into a nursing home and be determined by taking the funds in the trust and dividing them by them by the average monthly nursing home bill as established by the welfare department in their state. The ineligibility occurs because the state considers the taking away the trustee's power to give principal and income to the donors to be a "transfer." I use the word "likely" because many states (New York and Massachusetts being the most prominent) outlawed them as against public policy.

After August 11, 1993, "trigger trusts" are ineffective. Technically, "trigger trusts" established before August 11, 1993 should be effective for now. However, as previously mentioned, more and more states are prohibiting their use retroactively. Be sure to have any trust you had drafted prior to August 11, 1993 to protect assets reviewed by a competent elder law attorney.

Example 3 An "indirect irrevocable" trust

Mr. and Mrs. Andrews set up a trust with their children as beneficiaries, and their son as trustee. Under the terms of the trust the beneficiaries can receive income or principal at the discretion of the trustee. The trust terminates at the death of the surviving parent and all assets are distributed to the children.

Under the old law you rarely saw these types of trusts because the parents would not give up control. Rather you saw "income only" instruments.

Opinion:

Under the 1993 law, you may see more of these trusts because individuals will not want to take the chance that "income–only" instruments will be declared invalid.

This type of trust should protect assets since the parents are not beneficiaries. However, there are some cautions:

First, you must be very careful not to use this instrument as your private bank. Medicaid will look not only at withdrawals from an applicant's accounts over the past 3 years but also at deposits. They will interpret excessive "gifts" from your children deposited into your bank account as a sign that you did not give up control of those funds even though you are not listed as a beneficiary

Second, Medicaid may rule that your trust is really a "to or for the benefit of" trust. In other words,you never intended to give up control, as is proved by your appointing your child as trustee and having beneficiaries make "gifts" to you on a regular basis.

In that case, they may apply a 5-year look–back period. Remember, however, the ineligibility will probably be less than the applicable look–back periods. See this chapter for a complete explanation of "look–back" and ineligibility periods A straight irrevocable trust is effective if you understand that those assets are "frozen." It should hold only thosc assets that you have not touched and do not plan on touching (i.e. a summer home or stocks and bonds).

What should the Andrews do?

Scenario 1

Total countable assets: $50,000

Income: Husband, $650 *per month; wife,* $300 *per month*

1997 minimum for community spouse ("floor"): $15,804

1997 maximum for community spouse ("ceiling"): $79,020

State formula for deciding how much community spouse keeps: Total countable assets divided by 2. If one half is between "floor" and "ceiling", he/she keeps that amount.

At risk: One half or $25,000

Average cost of nursing home care in their state: $3,500

The proper approach is to do nothing, because even though $25,000 is at risk, Mrs. Andrews would be allowed to keep her husbands spend–down of

$25,000 to generate income to help bring her up to the monthly minimum needs allowance, which in 1997 is $1,326.25. Please reivew the Resource-First provisions in Chapter 2.

Scenario 2

Total countable assets: $150,000

1997 minimum for community spouse ("floor"): $15,804

1997 maximum for community spouse ("ceiling"): $79,020

State formula for deciding how much community spouse keeps: Total countable assets divided by 2. If one half is between "floor" and "ceiling", he/she keeps that amount.

At risk: All countable assets above $79,020: $70,980

Average cost of nursing home care in their state: $3,500

The suggestion in this scenario is also to do nothing because of the Resource-First Rule. Here's how it works:

1. The community spouse, Mrs. Andrews, is allowed to keep an MMNA of $1,326.25 (1997). Her monthly income is only $300. Therefore she is short $1,026.25.
2. Medicaid will attribute a return on her spousal allowance, generally using current short–term interest rates. Let's say that's 5%. Five percent of $79,020 is about $329 per month. This added to her $300 per month in Social Security benefits equals $629 per month. She is still short $697.25 per month.
3. Medicaid will allow the communtiy spouse to keep whatever is necessary from Mr. Andrews's spend–down of $70,980 to generate $697.25 per month. Assuming the same rate of return, only $3,549 per year, or $296 per month would be generated.

Therefore under the above scenario, Mrs. Andrews would be allowed to keep her husbands spend–down and her allowance for a total of $150,000. Since she is still short of the $1,326.25 MMNA, she can then go to her husband's monthly income to make up the difference.

Scenario 3

Total countable assets: $80,000

1997 minimum for community spouse ("floor"): $15,804

1997 maximum for community spouse ("ceiling"): $79,020

State formula for deciding how much community spouse keeps: Their state has raised the "floor" to $79,020.Total countable assets divided by 2. If onc half is between "floor" and "ceiling" he/she keeps that amount. If "floor" is "ceiling" he/she keeps the maximum amount.

At risk: $3,980

Average cost of nursing home care in their state: $3,500

In this cxample no Medicaid planning is suggested because the state has raised the "floor" to $79,020 and therefore the community spouse may keep this amount.

A note about the Andrews' house:

It makes no sense to protect the Andrews' money without protecting the house, too. Even though it is a non–countable asset (Medicaid allows the Andrews to keep it while receiving financial assistance), Medicaid will place a lien on the house upon the death of both spouses. Please refer to Chapter 6 for a complete explanation of how to protect a house.

Offspring and parents

This example deals with elderly parents who are both in frail health. The O'Connors have a close and trusting relationship with their children; therefore the children are available to help their parents protect their assets.

NAME:	Mr. and Mrs. O'Connor	
CHILDREN:	Maria and Joseph	
PARENTS' AGES:	husband: 82 wife: 79	
ASSETS:	two–family house	$150,000
	savings bonds	$75,000
	stocks	$75,000
	savings and CDs:	$40,000
INCOME:	husband: $1000/month social security, $800/month pension wife: $550 /month social security, $150/month pension joint: $350/month investment interest	
HEALTH:	husband: Parkinson's disease, early stage wife: fair	

Our goal is to make sure sufficient assets remain to pay for Mr. O'Connor's care.

Here's how the assets line up before steps are taken to protect them:

non–countable	**countable**	**inaccessible**
Two–family house	savings and CDs $44,000 stocks $75,000 savings bonds $75,000	none currently

Let's look at the various options to protect assets when Mr. O'Connor has time to plan. Remember, he does not need 3 years, only enough time to cover the ineligibility created by transferring his assets. Assets may be protected by:

Option 1 **Giving away assets to the offspring**

Option 2 **Holding them in trust**

Option 3 **Consider the Resource-First Rule (see Chapter 2).**

After examining each option, we will see which is best suited for this specific situation.

Option 1 Giving away assets to the offspring

Drawbacks

Here's what you want to avoid:

- The children's spending your money because they "thought it was a gift"
- Your son's or daughter's spouse's (whom you never liked in the first place) getting your assets in a divorce
- Your son's or daughter's losing the money in a bad business deal.
- Your son's or daughter's death.
- If assets that have a low cost basis, such as stock, are given away, the children receive that basis. When the asset is sold there will be a large capital gain. However if the stock remains in the your name, there will be a free cost "step–up" to fair market value when you die. Result: No capital gains tax for the children if they sell the stock.
- If assets are in qualified plans such as IRAs, transferring them means the possibility of penalties and steep income tax consequences.

- Loss of financial aid. If assets are given to children, and they have kids who receive financial aid in private school or college, that aid will probably be jeopardized.

Option 2 Holding assets in trust

The use of a Medicaid Qualifying Trust will not protect assets. The people who establish such an instrument are its beneficiaries and give discretion over the income and principal to the trustee. Please review Chapter 2.

Income–only trusts, discussed below, may work, but read further.

As of August 11, 1993, owing to the passage of new laws contained in the Omnibus Budget Reconciliation Act (OBRA '93), the use of any type of trust, once a basic tool for protecting assets from Medicaid, has been severely restricted. Let's look at several examples of trusts, with an opinion at the end of each one as to whether it will work in this example since the law has changed. For a complete explanation, see Chapter 2.

Example 1 An irrevocable "income–only" trust

The O'Connors set up the O'Connor Family Trust with their children as trustees and themselves as beneficiaries. They do not give the trustees the power to give them assets, only the power to hold assets in trust while they generate income for their parents. Let's assume the applicable ineligibility period has passed (funds transferred into the trust divided by the average monthly nursing home bill. The day Mr. O'Connor goes into the nursing home is the day the snapshot is taken of their assets. The assets in the trust are not in the snapshot because the trustees cannot make them available to beneficiaries.

Opinion:

Prior to OBRA '93, the principal in this instrument would be protected as long as the ineligibility period had run. One half of the net income, however, would be available to the spouse entering the nursing home.

Under the new law, it is likely that income–only trusts will still protect principal. The actual answer is still open to debate among lawyers. See Chapter 2 for a full explanation. Even if assets are protected, there is still a chance your state may get them after the death of the donors through a procedure called estate recovery.

Example 2 A "trigger" trust

Mr. and Mrs. O'Connor set up a trust with their children as beneficiaries and one of them, Maria, as trustee. The parents can get principal and income from the trust while both of them are healthy. However, should one of them become ill in the future or go into a nursing home, a change is triggered under the terms of the trust: the trustee is then ordered not to give either parent principal or income and instead to make those funds available to the beneficiaries (the two children.) The parents would be ineligible for Medicaid based on the amount of the transfer (funds transferred divided by the average monthly nursing home bill) but not more than 30 months if established prior to August 11, 1993, or 3 years after that date, but thereafter either or both would have qualified.

Opinion:

Prior to OBRA '93, it was likely that this type of trust would protect assets and income after the ineligibility period ran. It would begin on the day of entry into a nursing home and be determined by taking the funds in the trust and dividing them by the average monthly nursing home bill as established by the welfare department in their state. The ineligibility occurs because the state considers the taking away the trustee's power to give principal and income to the donors to be a "transfer." I use the word "likely" because many states (New York being the most prominent) outlawed "trigger trusts" as against public policy.

After OBRA '93, "trigger trusts" offer dubious protection. Technically, "trigger trusts" established before August 11, 1993 should be effective. However, as previously mentioned, more and more states are prohibiting their use retroactively. Be sure to have any trust you had drafted to protect assets reviewed by competent counsel.

Example 3 An "indirect irrevocable" trust

Mr. and Mrs. O'Connor set up a trust with their children as beneficiaries and their daughter as trustee. Under the terms of the trust the beneficiaries can receive income or principal at the discretion of the trustee. The trust terminates at the death of the surviving parent and all assets are distributed to the children.

Prior to OBRA '93, you rarely saw these types of trusts because the parents would not give up control. Rather you saw "income–only" instruments.

Opinion:

Under the new law, you may see more of these trusts because individuals will not want to take the chance that "income–only" instruments will be declared invalid.

What will work best for the O'Connors?

Total countable assets: $190,000

1997 minimum for community spouse ("floor"): $15,804

1997 maximum for community spouse ("ceiling): $79,020

Income: Husband, $1,800*; wife,* $800

At risk: All countable assets over $79,020, or $113,980

Average cost of nursing home care in their state: $3,500

The suggestion in this scenario is to use the Resource-First Rule first. Here's how it works:

1. The community spouse, Mrs. O'Connor, is allowed to keep a MMNA of $1,326.25 (1997). Her monthly income is only $800. Therefore, she is short $526.25.

2. Medicaid will attribute a return on her spousal allowance, generally using current short–term interest rates. Let's say that's 5%. Five percent of $79,020 is about $329 per month. This added to her $800 per month in Social Security benefits equals $1129 per month. She is still short $197.25 per month;

3. Medicaid will allow the communtiy spouse to keep whatever is necessary from Mr. O'Connor's spend–down of $110,980 to generate $197.25 per month. Assuming the same rate of return, Mrs. O'Connor could keep approximately $48,000 of her husband's spend–down. She therefore keeps $127,020. What's at risk is $62,980.

Since Mrs. O'Connor can keep most of the couple's life savings,and prepay her and her husband's funerals (figure about $12,000), it is advised that she spend at least $30,000 to preserve her choice of a nursing home should her husband need one. The balance of $20,980 can be transferred to her children. The ineligibility period is determined by dividing these funds by the average monthly cost of nursing home care as established by the state the O'Connors live in. If that amount is $3,000, the disqualification period would be just under 7 months.

Warning: Please remember to review the Kennedy-Kassebaum law in the section "The ineligibility period" of Chapter 3. It appears to prohibit these types of transfers. Furthermore, be advised that at the time this book went to press, a bill had been introduced to repeal the above criminal sanctions. Please check with a competent attorney to determine the status of the effort.

A note about the O'Connors' house: It makes no sense to protect their money without protecting the house too. Even though it is a non–countable asset (Medicaid allows them to keep it while receiving financial assistance), a lien will be placed on the house upon the death of both spouses. Please refer to Chapter 6 for a complete explanation of how to protect a house.

Offspring and single parent

This example is used to show how children can help a widowed parent who suffers from a debilitating illness protect her assets.

NAME:	Mrs. Lawrence
CHILDREN:	one daughter, Ruth (married)
AGE:	86
ASSETS:	savings: $75,000
INCOME:	social security: $400/month investments: $500/month
HEALTH:	early stage Alzheimer's

The goal is to protect countable assets from being spent on Mrs. Lawrence's nursing home confinement.

Here's how the assets line up before steps are taken to protect them:

non–countable	**countable**	**inaccessible**
none	$75,000	none currently

What should Mrs. Lawrence do?

If assets remain in the countable column, they will have to be spent on nursing home care before Mrs. Lawrence can qualify for benefits.

If these assets are transferred to the inaccessible column within 3 years of applying for Medicaid, they presume the transfer was made to qualify for assistance. The resulting ineligibility period is determined by taking the value of assets transferred and dividing them by the average monthly cost of nursing home care as established by Medicaid. See this chapter. Let's see what options are available:

Remember, assets may be protected (made inaccessible) by:

Option 1 Giving them away

Option 2 Holding them in trust

After examining each option, we will see which is best suited for this specific situation.

Option 1 Giving away assets

If her savings account is held jointly with her daughter, Mrs. Lawrence can simply take off her name and social security number. Doing so creates an ineligibility period because Medicaid considers it a transfer of assets. If the account is in her name alone, the money can be transferred to an account with only her daughter's name and social security number. If Mrs. Lawrence can avoid applying for Medicaid during the ineligibility period created by the transfer (funds transferred divided by the average monthly nursing home bill established by her state welfare department), the money is protected.

Drawbacks

- Ruth may think the assets are a gift and may spend them.
- Ruth may get a divorce.
- Ruth may lose the money in a bad business deal.
- Ruth may die.
- Ruth's children may lose financial aid for college.
- If assets with a low cost basis, such as stock, are given away, Ruth will receive that basis. When the assets are sold there will be a large capital gain. However, if the stock remains in Mrs. Lawrence's name, there will be a free cost "step–up" to fair market value when they die. Result: No capital gains tax for Ruth if she sells the stock.
- If assets are in qualified plans such as IRAs, transferring them means the possibility of penalties and steep income tax consequences.

Option 2 Holding assets in trust

The use of a Medicaid Qualifying Trust will not protect assets. The people who establish such an instrument are its beneficiaries and give discretion over the income and principal to the trustee. Please review Chapter 2.

Income–only trusts, discussed below, may work, but read further.

As of August 11, 1993, owing to the passage of new laws contained in the Omnibus Budget Reconciliation Act (OBRA '93), the use of any type of trust, once a basic tool for protecting assets from Medicaid, has been severely restricted. Let's look at several examples of trusts, with an opinion at the end of each one as to whether they will work in this example since the law has changed. For a complete explanation, see Chapter 2.

Example 1 An irrevocable "income–only" trust

Mrs. Lawrence sets up the Lawrence Family Trust with her daughter as trustees and herself as beneficiary. She does not give the trustee the power to give her assets, only the power to hold them in trust while they generate income for Mrs. Lawrence. Let's assume the applicable ineligibility period has passed (funds transferred into the trust divided by the average monthly nursing home bill; see Chapter 3). The assets in the trust are not counted because the trustee cannot make them available to Mrs. Lawrence.

Opinion:

Prior to OBRA '93, the principal in this instrument would be protected as long as the ineligibility period had run. The net income, however, would be available to Mrs. Lawrence and therefore to the nursing home.

Under the new law, it is likely that income–only trusts will still protect principal. Even if assets are protected there is still a chance your state may get them after the death of the donor through a procedure called estate recovery. See Chapter 2.

Example 2 A "trigger" trust

Mrs. Lawrence sets up a trust with her daughter Ruth and grandchildren as beneficiaries and Ruth as the Trustee. Mrs. Lawrence can get principal and income from the trust while she is out of a nursing home. However, should she go into a nursing home, a change is triggered under the terms of the trust: The trustee is then ordered not *to give Mrs. Lawrence principal or income and instead to make those funds available to the other beneficiaries. Mrs. Lawrence would then be ineligible for Medicaid based on the amount of money that was transferred into the trust (funds transferred divided by the average monthly nursing home bill) but not more than 30 months if set up prior to August 11, 1993, or 3 years if set up after that.*

Opinion:

Prior to OBRA '93, it was likely that this type of trust would protect assets and income after the ineligibility period ran. It would begin on the day of entry into a nursing home and be determined by taking the funds in the trust and dividing them by by the average monthly nursing home bill as established by the welfare department in her state. The ineligibility occurs because the state considers the taking away of the trustee's power to give principal and income to the donor to be a "transfer". I use the word "likely" because many states (New York being the most prominent) outlawed "trigger trusts" as against public policy.

After August 11, 1993, "trigger trusts" are ineffective. Technically, "trigger trusts" established before August 11, 1993 should still be effective. However, as previously mentioned, more and more states are prohibiting their use retroactively. Be sure to have any trust you had drafted to protect assets reviewed by a competent elder law attorney.

Example 3 An "indirect irrevocable" trust

Mrs. Lawrence sets up a trust with her daughter and grandchildren as beneficiaries, and her daughter as trustee. Under the terms of the trust the beneficiaries can receive income or principal at the discretion of the trustee. The trust terminates at Mrs. Lawrence's death and all assets are distributed to the beneficiaries.

Prior to OBRA '93, you rarely saw these types of trusts because the parent would not give up control. Rather you saw "income–only" instruments.

Opinion:

Under the new law, it is likely you will see more of these trusts because lawyers will not want to take the chance that "income–only" instruments will be declared invalid.

What trust will work best for the Lawrences? Probably the "indirect irrevocable" trust.

Mrs. Lawrence sets up the Lawrence Family Irrevocable Trust with her daughter, Ruth, as trustee and Ruth and her children as beneficiaries. Mrs. Lawrence is not the beneficiary and therefore cannot receive any income or principal from the trust. As the trustee, Ruth is given discretion over both income and principal and can distribute it to any of the beneficiaries at any time.

This type of trust should protect assets since Mrs. Lawrence is not a beneficiary. However, there are some cautions: First, you must be very careful not to use this instrument as your private bank. Medicaid will look not only at withdrawals from an applicant's accounts over the past 3 years but also at deposits. They will interpret excessive "gifts" from your children deposited into your bank account as a sign that you did not give up control of those funds even though you are not listed as a beneficiary. Second, Medicaid may rule that your trust is really a "to or for the benefit of" trust. In that case, they may apply a 5-year look–back period which could put those assets at risk. Remember, however, the ineligibility will probably be far less than 36 or 60 months. See this chapter for a complete explanation of "look–back" and ineligibility periods. A straight irrevocable trust is effective if you understand that those assets are "frozen." It should hold only those assets that you have not touched in years.

Warning: Please remember to review the Kennedy-Kassebaum law in the section "The ineligibility period" of Chapter 3. It appears to prohibit these types of transfers. Furthermore, be advised that at the time this book went to press, a bill had been introduced to repeal the above criminal sanctions. Please check with a competent attorney to determine the status of the effort.

The decision on whether to place assets in trust or give them away is hers. The question is how much. Let's assume that Mrs. Lawrence needs at least $25,000 to get into a good nursing home. Add to that a pre–paid funeral (about $5,000) and her cash allowance (usually $2,000) and you come to approximately $32,000. Subtract this from $75,000 and you get $43,000. Consider transferring this amount. The ineligibility period is determined by taking funds transferred divided by the average monthly nursing home bill as established by the department of welfare ($3,000 in this example). Mrs. Lawrence could not apply for Medicaid until almost 15 months had passed. She would use the remaining funds to get into a good facility and buy a funeral.

Warning! As discussed in Chapter 3, under the new Kennedy–Kassebaum bill transfers of assets that create a period of ineligibility could trigger criminal sanctions. Please review this statute thoroughly.

When siblings have time to plan

This example is used to show the dangers of holding assets jointly with siblings and how one sibling can help the other protect assets.

Medicaid presumes that the person applying for assistance owns all the funds. Unless the co–owner can prove some or all belong to her, they will be lost. For a complete explanation, see Chapter 4.

NAME:	Ethel and Coretta Johnson	
AGE:	81 and 77, respectively	
ASSETS:	CDs:	$75,000
	bonds	$100,000
	two–family house	$150,000
	(all above held jointly)	
	insurance, whole life, held by Ethel	
	cash surrender value	$10,000
INCOME:	Ethel's social security:	$750/month
	Coretta's social security:	$700/month
	joint, from investments:	$520/month
HEALTH:	Ethel has been in poor health for years and has a history of heart problems	
	Coretta is in good health	

The goal is to place aside enough money to pay for Ethel's care but to have enough to provide for Coretta.

Here's how the assets line up:

non–countable	countable	inaccessible
two–family house	$100,000 bonds	none currently
	$75,000 CDs	
	whole life policy, cash surrender value $10,000	

If assets remain in the countable column, they will have to be spent down on nursing home care before Ethel qualifies for financial assistance. If they are transferred to the inaccessible column within 3 years of going into a nursing home, Medicaid presumes that Ethel was trying to protect the assets and she will not qualify for assistance until the ineligibility period runs on the transfer. Let's look at the various options.

Remember, assets may be protected by:

Option 1 Giving them away

Option 2 Holding them in trust

After examining each option, we will see which is best suited for this specific situation.

The use of a Medicaid Qualifying Trust will not protect assets. The people who establish such an instrument are its beneficiaries and give discretion over the income and principal to the trustee. Please review Chapter 2.

Income–only trusts, discussed below, may work, but read further.

As of August 11, 1993, owing to the passage of new laws contained in the Omnibus Budget Reconciliation Act (OBRA '93), the use of any type of trust, once a basic tool for protecting assets from Medicaid, has been severely restricted. Let's look at several examples of trusts ,with an opinion at the end of each one as to whether they will work in this example since the law has changed. For a complete explanation, see Chapter 2.

Example 1 An irrevocable "income–only" trust

Ethel Johnson could set up the Johnson Family Trust with her sister as trustee and herself as beneficiary. She does not give the trustee the power to give her assets, only the power to hold them in trust while they generate income for her. Let's assume the applicable ineligibility period has passed (funds transferred into the trust divided by the average monthly nursing home bill; see Chapter 2). The assets in the trust are not counted because the trustees cannot make them available to beneficiaries.

Opinion:

Prior to OBRA '93, the principal in this instrument would be protected as long as the ineligibility period had run. The net income, however, would be available to Ethel once she is on Medicaid.

Under the new law, it is likely that income–only trusts will still protect principal. The actual answer is still open to debate among lawyers. Even if assets are protected, however, there is still a chance your state may get them after the death of the donors through a procedure called estate recovery. See Chapter 2.

Example 2 A "trigger" trust

Ethel sets up a trust with her sister as beneficiary and trustee. Ethel can get principal and income from the trust while she is healthy. However, should she become ill in the future or go into a nursing home, a change is triggered under the terms of the trust: The trustee is then ordered not *to give Ethel principal or income and instead to make those funds available to Coretta. Ethel would be ineligible for Medicaid based on the amount of the transfer (funds transferred divided by the average monthly nursing home bill) but not for more than 30 months. If the trust was established prior to August 11, 1993, or 3 years after that date, but thereafter either or both would have qualified.*

Opinion:

Prior to OBRA '93, it was likely that this type of trust would protect assets and income after the ineligibility period ran. It would begin on the day of entry into a nursing home and be determined by taking the funds in the trust and dividing them by the average monthly nursing home bill as established by the welfare department in their state. The ineligibility occurs because the state considers the taking away of the trustee's power to give principal and income to the donors to be a "transfer." I use the word "likely" because many states (New York being the most prominent) outlawed "trigger trusts" as being against public policy.

After August 11, 1993, "trigger trusts" are ineffective. Technically, "trigger trusts" established before August 11, 1993 should be effective at this time. However, as previously mentioned, more and more states are prohibiting their use retroactively. Be sure to have any trust you had drafted to protect assets reviewed by a competent elder law attorney.

In any case, this kind of trust is useless because Ethel is already sick.

Example 3 An "indirect irrevocable" trust

Ethel sets up a trust with Coretta as beneficiary and trustee. Under the terms of the trust the beneficiary can receive income or principal at the discretion of the trustee. Coretta can distribute income or principal to herself. The trust terminates at Ethel's death and all assets are distributed to Coretta or whomever else Ethel decides should get her money.

Prior to OBRA '93, you rarely saw these types of trusts because the donor would not give up control. Rather you saw "income–only" instruments.

Opinion:

Under the new law, it is likely you will see more of these trusts because lawyers will not want to take the chance that "income–only" instruments will be declared invalid.

What trust will work best for the Johnsons? Probably the "indirect irrevocable" trust.

Ethel sets up the Johnson Family Irrevocable Trust with her sister as trustee and beneficiary. Ethel is not the beneficiary and therefore cannot receive any income or principal from the trust. As the trustee, Coretta is given discretion over both income and principal and can distribute it to herself at any time.

This type of trust should protect assets since Ethel is not a beneficiary. However, there are some cautions: First, she must be very careful not to use this instrument as her private bank. Medicaid will look not only at withdrawals from an applicant's accounts over the past 3 years but also at deposits. They will interpret excessive "gifts" from Coretta deposited into Ethel's bank account as a sign that she did not give up control of those funds even though she is not listed as a beneficiary. Second, Medicaid may rule that the trust is really a "to or for the benefit of" trust (see Chapter 2). In that case, they will apply a 60–month look–back period (as opposed to 3 years) which could put those assets at risk. Remember, however, the ineligibility will probably be far less than 36 or 60 months. A straight irrevocable trust is effective if you understand that those assets are "frozen." It should hold only those funds that you have not touched in years.

Warning: Please review the Kennedy–Kassebaum bill in the section "The ineligibility period" of Chapter 3. It appears that it may be illegal to transfer money into a trust, if the purpose is to qualify for Medicaid. Furthermore, be advised that at the time this book went to press, a bill had been introduced to repeal the above criminal sanctions. Please check with a competent attorney to determine the status of the effort.

What should the Johnsons do?

> *Total countable assets:* $135,000 (CDs, bonds and cash surrender value on Ethel's whole life insurance.
>
> *At risk:* All jointly held assets are considered available to Ethel if she applies for Medicaid subject to Coretta's proving that they belong to her.
>
> *Average cost of nursing home care in her state:* $4,000

The decision on whether to place assets in trust or give them away is theirs. The question is how much. First Coretta must get Ethel's name off her assets. There is no ineligibility attached to the transfer if Coretta can prove that they are her assets. Let's assume that her share is $60,000. The balance of $75,000 is available to spent on Ethel's care.

Let's also assume that she will need at least $25,000 to get into a good nursing home. Add to that a prepaid funeral (about $5,000) and her cash allowance (usually $2,000) and you come to approximately $32,000. Subtract this from $75,000 and you get $43,000.

Consider transferring this amount either into a trust or simply give it away to Coretta. The ineligibility period is determined by taking funds transferred divided by the average monthly nursing home bill as established by the department of welfare ($3,000 in this example). Ethel could not apply for Medicaid until about 14 months passes. She would use the remaining funds to get into a good facility and prepay a funeral.

Warning! Please review the Kennedy–Kassebaum bill in Chapter 7.

A word about the Johnsons' house. Assuming it is held as joint tenants and not tenants in common, it will go to the surviving sister when one dies. Under present Medicaid law, no lien will be placed on the house because Coretta lives there. For a complete look at houses, please see Chapter 6.

Nieces/nephews and aunts/uncles

Protecting assets for these individuals can be accomplished using the same methods discussed in the "Lawrence" case.

Grandparents and grandchildren

Protecting assets for these individuals can be accomplished using the same methods discussed in the "Lawrence" case and the "Ethel and Coretta" case.

Unrelated people

Protecting assets for unrelated individuals can be accomplished using the same methods discussed in the "Ethel and Coretta" case.

CHAPTER 4

WHAT TO DO WHEN YOU DON'T HAVE TIME TO PROTECT YOUR ASSETS

WHAT TO DO WHEN YOU DON'T HAVE TIME TO PROTECT YOUR ASSETS

There *is* something you can do!

The whole concept of planning hinges on the disqualification period. Protecting assets even if you don't have time to plan can be accomplished if you grasp the following statement:

"If a person makes a transfer of countable assets for less than fair market value within 3 years of applying for Medicaid (60 months if the transfer was to or from certain types of trusts [see Chapter 2]), it is presumed that the transfer was made to have Medicaid pay the nursing home bills."

The 3 years is referred to as the "look–back period." In other words, Medicaid has the right to look back 3 years from the date of an application for Medicaid benefits. If a transfer was made to certain types of trusts, the period is extended to 60 months. What confuses many people is that they think the look–back period is the actual amount of time they are disqualified from receiving Medicaid benefits because they made a transfer of assets, no matter how small. This is not the case!

Medicaid disqualifies the person going into a medical institution or nursing home for transferring only countable, not non–countable assets (see Chapter 2), With the exception of the house, non–countable assets may be transferred to anyone, at any time, even while applying for financial assistance.

Protecting countable assets

Understanding non–countable assets can give you a tool to protect some assets when your back is against the wall and you don't have 3 years to plan.

At first glance, this might not be apparent because the list of exempt assets is so limited. Generally, the only non–countable assets a person can keep are the following:

- A house used as a primary residence (in most states this includes two– and three–family homes)
- An amount of cash, usually $2,000
- A car
- Personal jewelry
- Household effects
- A pre–paid funeral
- A burial account (if allowed by your state)
- Term life (as opposed to whole life) insurance policies which have no cash surrender value

For more information on what your state considers to be non–countable assets, see Chapter 12.

With the exception of the house (see Chapter 6), most non–countable assets don't represent a lot of money. Their real value is that, in most states, they can be purchased with countable assets (funds from a savings account, for instance) at any time, even while applying for Medicaid. Medicaid allows you to spend countable assets on specified goods as long as they are for fair market value and non–countable. Fair market value is defined as the going rate for goods or services. For example in most states you could buy a reasonably priced car for the at–home spouse out of "countable" funds.

Medicaid penalizes the transfer of countable assets for other than fair market value. You can't take assets that would have to be spent on a medical institution or nursing home and get rid of them without receiving something of roughly equal value.

The same concept applies to the purchase of services. Household repairs such as replacing a leaking roof or fixing a noisy muffler in your car and various other necessary household expenses can be paid for out of a "countable" savings account, as long as the cost is consistent with the going rate.

A caution: Don't get too creative with this concept or you could get into a real pickle. There couldn't be a clearer example than a case recently decided in Massachusetts. A lawyer instructed his client to spend a great deal of cash on a diamond ring which he argued was personal jewelry, just as the person was going into a nursing home, believing that this was a way of protecting assets. When Medicaid balked, the case went to court. In arguing his case, the attorney quoted chapter and verse of the state regulation. The court didn't buy it. It held that the regulation exempting jewelry pertained to jewelry already owned by a Medicaid applicant.

The key idea here is to be reasonable. Medicaid officials just won't be impressed by purchases of expensive items like jewelry or oriental rugs. No state will accept such items as legitimate, non–countable household items.

Example: Robert, single, has $25,000 in a money market account and is going into a nursing home in the near future. If he transfers the money outright to his relatives and applies for assistance, the Medicaid office will do the following:

1. *Look back 3 years from the date of the application and question every withdrawal and deposit over about $1,000.*
2. *Assume that any large withdrawals were made for the purpose of protecting funds and that any large unexplained deposits come from some source that was not disclosed.*
3. *Determine the ineligibility period when Robert will be prohibited from receiving benefits. To do this they will take the funds transferred and divide the amount by the average monthly nursing home reimbursement established by the state welfare department. (For a complete explanation of look–back and ineligibility periods see Chapter 3.)*

Note that the above rule has come under attack. On January 1, 1997, the Health Insurance Portability Act, also known as the Kennedy–Kassebaum bill, went into effect. One section of that law appears to have effectively criminalized Medicaid planning. Contained in section 217, the provision is titled: "Criminal penalties for acts involving Medicare or State health care programs (Medicaid)." It states:

"Whoever...knowingly and willfully disposes of assets (including by any transfer in trust) in order for an

individual to become eligible for medical assistance (Medicaid) under a State plan under title XIX, if disposing of the assets results in the imposition of a period of ineligibility for such assistance shall...be punishable by a fine of up to $10,000 and or up to one year in jail." In addition your state could disqualify you from Medicaid benefits for up to one year.

There are, as of this writing, two interpretations:

1. If you make any transfer within the look-back period, which is 3 years for outright transfers, and 60 months for transfers into a trust, you have violated the law.
2. The less restrictive interpretation is that if you wait for the ineligibility period to expire (as in the above example), no law has been violated.

The truth of the matter, however, is that no–one has any idea of how this statute will be interpreted. Furthermore, at the time this book went to press, a bill had been introduced to repeal the above criminal sanctions. It is essential that you consult with a competent attorney to determine the status of this repeal effort, to help you make decisions.

Most states will allow Robert to purchase a prepaid funeral and pay off legitimate bills such as charge cards and mortgages. There are lawyers who suggest buying expensive cars and making expensive additions to your house. This is questionable advice and Medicaid will probably disallow such expenditures.

Example: Edward and Mary have $50,000 in savings. They didn't have time to plan before Mary went into a nursing home on May 1. Under the law in most states, Edward can keep only one half of the assets (see Chapter 2). However, Mary is allowed to buy with her $25,000 a number of non–countable assets, as Robert could in our example above.

Let's take this example one step farther. In addition to the assets, Edward and Mary have a house with a $10,000 mortgage remaining on it and a car loan. The law allows Mary to pay off the entire mortgage and car loan from her funds only, assuming she signed on the notes.

The benefits are obvious. Mary can convert non–exempt assets to exempt assets. She can use funds which otherwise would go to the nursing home to pay off major debts and some lesser expenses such as a pre–paid funeral and some household items and repairs.

"...within 3 years of applying for Medicaid if transfers were outright, or within 60 months for transfers to or from certain types of trusts..."

Medicaid will question every withdrawal or deposit typically over $1,000 if made within the look–back period. They will also examine your deposits to see if they indicate undisclosed assets. On the other hand Medicaid cannot look back more than the period allowed by law which we discussed above. Therefore, if you simply transfer funds and let the look–back period expire you will thereafter qualify for Medicaid. You must be excruciatingly accurate because applying for benefits too early could mean the loss of all transferred funds. Here are two examples:

Example 1: For two years, Tom has been in a nursing home which costs $35,000 a year. He has $150,000 left. He has heard that he cannot transfer funds because he is already in a nursing facility.

That is not true in any state. If Tom transferred the entire $150,000 to his son, say, on January 1, 1997, and waited a full 3 years, he would thereafter qualify for Medicaid because he had not applied within the look–back period. His family would have to pay for three years of nursing home care, but they could keep whatever was left over. There may be tax advantages as well for the family during that period. The person paying the bill may be able to claim the expense as a medical deduction under section 213 of the Internal Revenue Code. An accountant or CPA can help you with this.

Example 2: Let's say the facts are the same as in Example 1 except for one thing: this time Tom applies for Medicaid December 29, 1999, just one day short of 3 years. Under rules that went into effect on August 11, 1993, the ineligibility period for Tom will not be just one day as it was before the law changed. The state will determine his ineligibility by dividing the funds transferred by the average monthly nursing home bill prevailing in the state. If, for example, Tom's state sets that figure at $2,500 a month, his ineligibility period would be 60 months, of which he has run just one day short of 3 years. He therefore has another 24 months to go before he qualifies for assistance from Medicaid! For a detailed explanation see Chapter 3.

"...it is presumed that the transfer was made to have Medicaid pay the nursing home bills."

Medicaid presumes that the transfer of countable assets for less than fair market value within 3 years of applying for Medicaid if an outright transfer, or within 60 months of applying for Medicaid in the case of transfers to or from certain types of trusts was made to protect those assets. Any presumption can be rebutted. In most states (make sure you check with your Department of Public Welfare), if you can show that at the time the transfer was made there was a legitimate reason for the transfer, those assets are protected and do not have to be spent as countable assets.

Here is a list of what most states consider to be legitimate transfers:

1. At the time countable assets were given away, you were in good health with no medical history of the illness that put you in a nursing home.
2. You had established a pattern of making transfers or gifts, such as reducing the size of your estate for tax purposes, or helping your grandchildren pay for college.
3. At the time you made the transfer or gift, you retained enough countable assets to pay for your then–anticipated medical expenses.

4. At the time you made the transfer or gifts, you were not, nor was your family, aware of the Medicaid regulations on transfer of assets.

Example: Roger, a divorced father of two college–age children, has a savings account of $150,000. For the past three years, he has contributed $10,000 per year to each child ($60,000 total) for college expenses. He has no record of major health problems.

Roger suffers a stroke which necessitates immediate nursing home care. He is allowed to take cash from his savings account ($90,000) and buy non–countable assets. Moreover, if his offspring can prove any one or all of the above criteria, they may not have to give the tuition money back to their father to be spent as a countable asset, and Roger will qualify for financial assistance.

These criteria apply to anyone, single or married, who makes a gift or spends countable assets within 3 years of applying for Medicaid. The disqualification period may be less based upon the amount transferred.

A note about gift taxes

There are two types of gift taxes: state and federal. Many people are confused about how much money they can give away without owing a federal gift tax.

They mistakenly believe they can only give away $10,000 a year. That's incorrect. Federal gift taxes only affect a person who has more than $600,000. In other words, if you have assets of less than $600,000 you can give away more than $10,000 a year, (even $599,999!) without owing a federal gift tax.

That's because we all start out with a credit at the IRS of $192,800 which represents the tax on a gift of $600,000. It's called a "unified" credit because it can be used to offset tax obligations created by gifts of more than $10,000 a year per person *or* death taxes on estates of up to $600,000 ($1.2 million per couple).

Yes, you do incur tax obligations on gifts over $10,000 per year per person. But if your assets are under $600,000 ($1.2 million per couple) it is wiped out by the unified credit. In other words don't worry about gift taxes for amounts over $10,000 per year unless your individual assets are over $600,000 or twice that for a couple (see Chapter 11, Tax Considerations).

This credit does not apply to taxes that your state may levy on gifts. Be sure to check with your state Department of Revenue.

Special cases

If you are holding your assets jointly with someone, there are a number of ways your account might be set up. The following is a list of commonly used titles on investments:

1. A in trust for B
2. A payable on death (POD) to B
3. A or B as tenants in common
4. A and B as joint tenants with right of survivorship

Here's how Medicaid generally regards these accounts: In numbers 1 and 2, A (typically a parent, grandparent or sibling) owns 100% of the account, not B. If B goes into the nursing home, the money is not considered his.

In number 3, the money usually belongs to the person who goes into the nursing home first, regardless of whose name is first. Your state, however, may consider only 50% of it available. Number 4 is considered an "and" account requiring two signatures. Generally, states treat these assets the same as number 3.

There are serious dangers in holding assets with a friend or a sibling. If he is institutionalized before you, Medicaid will presume that the assets belong entirely to him. The key word here is *presume.* In a crisis, most states (make sure to check with your elder law attorney) allow the co–holder to show that he either owns the assets or made a contribution to them in some proportion.

Evidence that can be presented includes a social security number on an account and records of deposits and withdrawals. Also helpful would be to show that the Medicaid applicant's signature was only on the account for convenience, as indicated through documents such as letters. In other words, if it's your money but the co–holder is institutionalized, you would be allowed to keep the money if you could show through evidence that in fact some or all of the money is yours.

You are well advised to look closely at how you are holding accounts, especially if you are single or widowed. Single parents tend to hold their money either with their children or siblings. If money is held with your children, it is considered 100% yours. If with your sibling, the money is considered 100% owned by the person who goes in first unless you can prove it's yours.

This can difficult. For example, if these funds were in a CD that had been rolled over for years, there may be no way of proving what funds are yours since there are no deposits or withdrawals.

Transfers between spouses and purchasing annuities

As previously discussed, Medicaid gives a degree of protection to the at–home or "community" spouse of a nursing home patient by allowing him or her to keep a certain amount of the couple's combined assets (see Chapter 2 for a complete explanation of the spousal allowance and Chapter 12 to determine what your state allows the at–home spouse to keep).

Although Medicaid permits unlimited transfers of countable assets between husband and wife, it would appear that there's no advantage to doing this because Medicaid lumps together all the couple's assets when determining eligibility.

However, there may be some advantage to so–called "front loading" assets into the name of the at–home spouse. Many states allow the at–home spouse to take countable assets and purchase a single premium immediate annuity. In other words, cash is turned into an income stream. As discussed earlier, income can be retained by the community spouse regardless of the amount. This provision, however, is controversial and there is little question that at some point in the near future the federal government will prohibit annuities as a way of protecting money from being spent on nursing home care. Be careful of anyone who suggests using annuities as a foolproof way of protecting your life savings.

Example: Edwin and Marge have $100,000 in countable assets. Marge needs nursing home care immediately. Upon admission, the nursing home will assess the couple's assets. Under the laws of the state where they live, Edwin is allowed to keep half or $50,000 and the balance will go to pay the nursing home.

Edwin, however, could transfer the entire $100,000 after the assessment is made and annuitize $50,000 of it in his name. He would then be allowed to keep the remaining $50,000.

There are several problems with this approach that have to considered:

1. By shifting the assets to the community spouse and annuitizing them, you are running the risk that

the community spouse may end up going into a nursing home. Since the annuity cannot be transferred or cashed in, you could lose all of the payout if the community spouse lives for a sufficiently long period of time once institutionalized.

2. If the assets of an unmarried parent are annuitized, although the parent would immediately qualify for Medicaid if institutionalized, the family would be placed in the position of a "death watch": the longer their parent lived, the more of the annuity would go to the nursing home, rather than to them as the beneficiaries upon the parent's death.
3. Some planners suggest that you tell the nursing home you have funds, which you may indeed have, for the purpose of getting your parent in. These planners tell you to wait until the nursing home commits to admitting your parent, and then annuitize. That is deceptive. It is wrong to promise a facility funds and then go back on your promise. The conduct is legal but the ethics are reprehensible.

Another problem: Edwin may live in a "cap" state, which means that if he someday needs a nursing home, he may never qualify for Medicaid because the income from the annuity plus his Social Security and other benefits put him over the cap (see Chapter 2 for a discussion on "cap states").

And the ultimate problem? States have the option, under current federal legislation, to prohibit the use of annuities for the purpose of protecting assets.

Using Supplemental Needs Trusts

Part of OBRA '93 legislation included the use of a special type of trust that holds money for disabled children under 65 of Medicaid applicants. Referred to as Supplemental Needs Trusts (SNTs), these instruments can be established even when an applicant or his or her spouse is requesting Medicaid benefits.

The trust must be established for a disabled child and provide that upon the child's death funds remaining in the trust be paid to the state, to reimburse it for benefits paid.

Spousal Refusal

There's another alternative to having one half or more of these assets spent on Edwin's care. Let's say that Marge, who now has all the money in her name only, refuses to give one half to the nursing home. This is called Spousal Refusal.

Congress envisioned circumstances in which a community spouse would not cooperate in a Medicaid application process, for example, he or she may be in parts unknown, separated from the applicant, or may simply want to hurt that person.

If the community spouse refuses to cooperate, Medicaid must qualify the applicant immediately. It requires, however, that Edwin give his rights to his marital assets to Medicaid. This is called an assignment of rights. If he does, Medicaid must qualify him for benefits immediately. However, if Edwin is unable to give the assignment because of incapacitation (such as a severe stroke), Medicaid will still qualify him for benefits.

Medicaid now has the right to sue Marge for those funds that should have been spent on Edwin's care.

So what's the purpose of this legal maneuver?

Based on Marge's age, health, and limited assets, it is possible that the court would give Marge a more generous division of assets than Medicaid regulations would allow.

Appealing Medicaid decisions on asset division

This option is available only to spouses. As we discussed earlier, a non–institutionalized spouse is allowed to keep an amount of money when the husband or wife goes into a chronic care facility or nursing home. This can range from a low of $15,804 to a maximum of $79,020 depending upon state regulations (see Chapter 12). The law does allow for an appeal for spouses who feel that the money they have left after asset division will not generate enough income to live on. If you believe that the assets left to the at–home spouse are not sufficient to generate income, you can ask for an appeals hearing through your local Department of Public Welfare.

Preserving "half-a-loaf"

We have previously discussed that Medicaid has a right to look at your previous financial transactions on the day you apply for assistance. You'll recall that they have a right to "look back" 3 years if there are outright transfers and 60 months for transfers to or from certain types of trusts (see Chapter 3). We have also seen that the period of ineligibility caused by transferring countable assets could be less than the look–back period. Under present law, it is possible to protect countable assets by transferring some of them and keeping enough funds aside to pay for the ineligibility period created by the transfer. Here's how that works:

Lawrence, in a nursing home for three years, has $60,000 left. The cost per month for his care is $3,000. His monthly income from social security is $1,000. If he transfers any money Medicaid will disqualify him based on the following formula: Funds transferred divided by the average monthly nursing home bill as set by Medicaid. Say he immediately transfers $60,000 to his children and applies for Medicaid. This is what will happen when he applies for assistance:

1. *Medicaid will look back 3 years to see if any transfers took place.*
2. *Medicaid will find the $60,000 transfer. The disqualification period will be determined by dividing the amount transferred ($60,000) by $3,000, which Lawrence's state considers to be the average monthly cost of care. The resulting figure, 20, is the number of months that Lawrence is ineligible for Medicaid. The problem of course is that he has no money left to pay for the ineligibility period.*

On the other hand, what if Lawrence transferred only $30,000? Divide that by $3,000 and you get only 10 months of ineligibility. The remaining $30,000, when combined with his monthly income from Social Security, should more than cover the actual cost ($3,000) of his care until the 10–month ineligibility period has run!

Note that the above rule has come under attack. On January 1, 1997, the Health Insurance Portability Act, also known as the Kennedy–Kassebaum bill, went into effect. One section of that law appears to have effectively criminalized Medicaid planning. Contained in section 217, the provision is titled:

"Criminal penalties for acts involving Medicare or State health care programs (Medicaid)." It states:

"Whoever...knowingly and willfully disposes of assets (including by any transfer in trust) in order for an individual to become eligible for medical assistance (Medicaid) under a State plan under title XIX, if disposing of the assets results in the imposition of a period of ineligibility for such assistance shall...be punishable by a fine of up to $10,000 and or up to one year in jail." In addition your state could disqualify you from Medicaid benefits for up to one year.

There are, as of this writing, two interpretations:

1. If you make any transfer within the look-back period, which is 3 years for outright transfers, and 60 months for transfers into a trust, you have violated the law.
2. The less restrictive interpretation is that if you wait for the ineligibility peirod to expire (as in the above example), no law has been violated.

The truth of the matter, however, is that no–one has any idea of how this statute will be interpreted. Furthermore, at the time this book went to press, a bill had been introduced to repeal the above criminal sanctions. It is essential that you consult with a competent attorney to determine the status of this repeal effort, to help you make decisions.

Suing your spouse for divorce

Under 1997 guidelines, the community spouse is allowed to keep from joint countable assets a maximum of $79,020. If that is not enough to provide for the community spouse, you may want to look at the possibility of a divorce on the theory that a divorce court will give you more of the marital assets than Medicaid would. Filing for a divorce is a terrible idea unless you have legitimate grounds.

Trying to get more assets because your spouse is going into a nursing home is, in my opinion, not one of them. Courts are loathe to grant divorces strictly on Medicaid grounds. Do not expect to get 100 percent of the marital assets after 50 years of marriage by simply saying, "I may lose them if my spouse stays in a nursing home."

CHAPTER 5

PROTECTING INCOME FROM MEDICAID

Spousal impoverishment guidelines

Most of an unmarried person's income cannot be protected from a nursing home or other long–term care institution. There are two exceptions: He or she may keep 1) a small personal needs account, and 2) premiums for health care coverage not paid for by Medicare (usually referred to as Medigap policies). However, Medicaid makes a provision for married couples that allows the at–home spouse to keep a portion of combined income.

Under federal guidelines, the at–home or "community" spouse (the person not going into the nursing home) can keep all of his or her income, regardless of the amount. However, if that monthly income falls below a federally mandated floor called a monthly minimum maintenance needs allowance (MMNA), which as of this writing (1997) is $1,326.25, then the community spouse can keep more of those assets of the institutionalized spouse that would otherwise have to be spent down.

The idea is to allow these extra assets to be retained so they could generate income which, when combined with the community spouse's monthly income, would bring the community spouse up to the MMNA.

Example: Louis and Mae are married with combined income of $2,000 (Louis's $1,200 and Mae's $800) and assets of $179,020. They live in a state which has not raised its MMNA above the federally mandated minimum of $1,326.25 for 1997.

If Louis needed nursing home care, Mae would be allowed to keep only $79,020 (see Chapter 3) plus the deductions described in Chapter 2. Louis would have to spend the balance, less these deductions. However since Mae's monthly income is less than the MMNA of $1,326.25, Medicaid will allow her to keep more of Louis's $100,000. Here's how it works:

1. *Medicaid imputes an interest for Mae's spousal share of $79,020. Let's say that interest rate is 5% per annum. The monthly income generated from this amount would be approximately $329.*
2. *Mae's monthly income is now $1,129. She is still $197.25 short of her MMNA of $1,326.25.*
3. *Medicaid will let Mae keep enough of Louis's spend–down to generate $197.25 per month. At the same interest rate of 5%, the capital required to do that is $47,340.*

The smaller Mae's monthly income, the more she could keep of her husband's assets. Finally, if there were not enough assets in Louis's spend–down figure to generate the extra monthly income from interest, Mae could use his monthly income to make up the difference.

The states have the authority to raise the MMNA "floor" to a maximum of $1,975.50 in 1997. Under federal rules, this number goes up every year.

Note: The state allows an at–home spouse to keep all her income including that earned from working and income from the assets she is allowed to keep. If Mae has monthly income from a part–time job of $1500, she does not have to give that money to her husband. However, she would not be able to keep any of her husbands spend-down. Our example uses a wife as the at–home spouse, but the rules apply just the same if the husband is at home.

Shelter Allowance

The at–home spouse may be entitled to additional monies (a shelter allowance) if she can show that the monthly maintenance allowance is insufficient to keep up her house. There is a formula that Medicaid uses to figure out the maximum additional allowance. The figuring is complicated and best explained by an example.

Walter is in a nursing home and has qualified for Medicaid. His monthly income is $1,500. His wife Nora continues to live at home. Her income is $450 from social security. The mortgage on the house is $700 per month and the utilities are $200 monthly.

Here are the steps that Nora should take to determine if she can get more than $1,326.25 a month.

1. *Add the monthly amount that Nora pays for her mortgage ($700) and utilities ($200), for a total of $900.*
2. *Take 30% of $1,326.25, Nora's standard monthly maintenance allowance. That amount is $397.88.*
3. *Deduct $397.88 from the total amount Nora pays for her mortgage and utilities ($900). $900 minus $397.88 equals $502.12, which is called her excess shelter allowance.*
4. *Add $502.12 to $1,326.25 = $1,828.37.*
5. *Deduct Nora's monthly income ($450) from $1,828.37 = $1,378.37.*

6. *The figure arrived at in step 5 is Nora's new monthly maintenance allowance.*

The question the community spouse must ask is: Do my monthly housing expenses eat up too much of my monthly maintenance allowance? Always assume that they do and use the above formula to see if you may be entitled to more than the minimum.

Remember: The only unquestioned increase that Medicaid allows in the monthly maintenance amount is to cover mortgage or rent and utilities.

Other ways to secure more income

Spouses who cannot survive financially on the allowance given to them by Medicaid can appeal directly to the state's welfare office. You must show that the income available is not sufficient to cover your needs because of unusual circumstances, e.g., high cost of maintaining a home. Be prepared to document your request. Basically, what the spouse is asking for is alimony (without a divorce) that federal law allows to be deducted from the institutionalized spouse's income.

"Miller" trusts

As previously mentioned in Chapter 2, approximately 25 states deny access to Medicaid benefits if an applicant's monthly income exceeds a certain amount. As of this writing (1997), that amount is $1,452. These are referred to as "cap states". The result can be devastating because no deductions are allowed from the net amount of an applicant's monthly income.

Colorado is a "cap state". One very smart attorney, Susan B. Haines, thought it manifestly unfair that people with no assets but decent monthly income should be denied Medicaid benefits because they were a few dollars over the cap. From this conviction came *Miller vs. Ibarra*. Ms. Haines submitted to the court a trust, and requested that the court order the payors of Miller's monthly income to pay that income to the trust. The instrument provided that the trustee could pay to Miller only an amount of monthly income that was less than the cap.

Colorado challenged the concept and lost. Under OBRA '93, the federal government adopted *Miller vs. Ibarra* as a way of allowing applicants whose income is in excess of the "cap" to qualify for benefits. This instrument is referred to as a "Miller trust" or "qualified income trust".

Here is what such a trust must provide:

1. The beneficiary must be the applicant.
2. The trust must provide that all of the applicant's income be paid directly to it.
3. The trust directs the trustee to distribute to the nursing home for the benefit of the applicant an amount of monthly income which is at least one dollar less than the existing "cap".
4. The trust must provide that at the death of the applicant, whatever is left be paid to the state.

A "Miller" trust may only be used in a "cap state".

Since this is a new planning tool, you are advised to consult with an elder law attorney, since your state may have a variation on the basic law.

CHAPTER 6

PROTECTING THE HOUSE – A VERY SPECIAL ASSET

Understanding the law

Every state has the power to place a lien on a person's home to recover the cost of nursing home care. Generally, the lien can only be placed on a home after the Medicaid recipient's death, assuming there is no surviving spouse or dependent child. Currently, a surviving spouse can remain in the house without a lien, making it possible for her to transfer the property to her children or anyone else.

The federal government gave the states the option of taking your house sooner rather than waiting until you die. A state can reclassify your house as a non–exempt asset if you are single, in a nursing home and cannot show that you'll be coming home within six months (see Chapter 12). The state may then insist that the house be sold to pay your nursing home bills, or it may take an assignment against your home; or if you refuse, your Medicaid benefits could be terminated.

Suppose your house is sold and the money is used to pay your nursing home bills. What happens if you recover and leave the nursing home? Good question. Bad news. You're homeless.

Prior to July 1, 1988, states had different interpretations of Medicaid regulations. Since Medicaid was funded half by the states and half by the federal government, each state was free to adopt rules that suited its particular circumstances. As a result, there was little uniformity, other than that the states could not be more restrictive than the basic guidelines set by the federal government.

Although the states agree on little, everyone seems to support the notion that a person's home is a very special asset that should be given certain protections that ordinary assets don't have. Most states allow the primary residence to remain a non–countable asset even if no one lives there. Many states used to allow the house to be transferred to family members or anyone else, not only within 30 months of requesting Medicaid, but even if the person making the transfer was on Medicaid!

But wait for a moment. Is it fair to allow a Medicaid recipient to transfer the house solely for the purpose of avoiding repayment of money paid on his or her behalf? Should we taxpayers be subsidizing inheritances? Most would answer a resounding "No" — with one exception: if the house being transferred belongs to a member of our family or a friend.

Congress realized that the states did not have the political backbone to prohibit these transfers. If any state representative voted to place a lien on a voter's property he wouldn't have a prayer of getting re–elected.

On July 1, 1988 and again on August 11, 1993 Congress mandated that the states adopt far–reaching regulations that will restrict the transfer of homes to children or relatives:

For single persons: A transfer of a primary residence to anyone, other than a protected class of persons, within the "look–back" period (see Chapter 3) will trigger an ineligibility period. The following are those to whom a house can be given without triggering an ineligibility period:

1. spouse.
2. a sibling who has had an equity interest in the property for at least one year.
3. a child who is either a minor, and/or is blind or disabled.
4. a child who has lived at the house for at least two years prior to his or her parent's entry into a nursing home and who has provided a level of care

which was instrumental in keeping that parent out of a nursing facility.

The actual time you are disqualified from receiving Medicaid will be determined by the value of the home (see Chapter 3, for the formula). As of August 11, 1993, transfers to certain types of trusts, could trigger a 5-year "look–back" period. It is critical that you thoroughly understand the consequences of transferring a home to a trust.

If you have your house in a revocable trust you will not qualify for Medicaid. If you transfer it back to you or your spouse, it becomes an available asset. If you transfer it to a third party, you may trigger a 5-year "look–back" period. The actual ineligibility would be determined by the value of the asset transferred divided by the average monthly nursing home bill as established by your state.

You are advised to check with competent counsel before doing so. Failure to understand the new penalty periods established by Congress as of August, 11, 1993 could end up costing you the entire value of your home even though it extends past the applicable "look–back" period.

Example: Leonard, who lives in Massachusetts, has a house worth $90,000. He transfers it to his sister for

$1.00 on January 1, 1997. Medicaid has established the average monthly nursing home bill at $4,500. The resulting ineligibility period is determined by a formula: the value of assets transferred ($90,000) divided by $4,500 or 20 months. Leonard must wait 20 months to qualify for Medicaid.

Since the transfer took place within the 36–month "look–back" period, Medicaid will ask Leonard, "What was the value of the home at the time you made the transfer?" The reply being $90,000, Medicaid divides that amount by a figure they established as an average monthly nursing home bill. In Massachusetts, in 1997, that's $4,500. The resulting ineligibility is 20 months, which means Leonard could apply one day after the 20 months expires. The "look–back" period is just that, a look back over the preceding 3 years from the date you apply for Medicaid.

Example: Leonard, who lives in Massachusetts, has a house worth $200,000. He transfers it to his sister for $1.00 on January 1, 1997. Medicaid has established the average monthly nursing home bill at $4,500. The resulting ineligibility is the value of assets transferred ($200,000) divided by $4,500, or just over 44 months. However, if Leonard does not apply for Medicaid *during the "look–back" period, which in 1997 is 3 years, he would thereafter qualify for Medicaid.*

Now here's the trap set by Congress on August 11, 1993. If anyone has an ineligibility period that is longer than 3 years (remember, take the value of assets transferred and divide it by your state's average monthly nursing–home bill established by Medicaid), and applies within the "look–back " period, then the disqualification will not be 3 years, but will be the actual period created by the transfer in the first place.

Example: Leonard has a house worth $200,000. He transfers it to his sister for $1.00 on January 1, 1997. Medicaid has established the average monthly nursing home bill at $4,500. The resulting ineligibility is the value of assets transferred ($200,000) divided by $4,500, or just over 44 months. Leonard applies for assistance on December 29, 1996, one day short of 3 years. Since he applied within the "look–back" period, he will not be eligible until another 8 months and one day have passed. Had he waited just one more day to apply, the application would have been beyond the "look–back" period of 3 years.

For couples: Either spouse is allowed to transfer, without penalty, his or her interest in their home to the other spouse at any time, even while on

Medicaid. Retransfer of the home to anyone, however, will trigger an ineligibility period.

New law: Medicaid provisions of the Omnibus Budget Reconciliation Act of 1993 (OBRA '93) implement mandatory recovery programs from a recipient's estate. An estate has traditionally been defined as any assets that are left in a person's name alone, or benefits or proceeds from investments that would be made payable to his estate upon his death.

The new law is vague as to what Medicaid may consider to be part of your estate. For example the law states an estate may include such "...assets conveyed to a survivor, heir, or assign of the deceased individual through joint tenancy, tenancy in common, survivorship, life estate, living trust, or other arrangements."

A traditional interpretation of "estates" would not include assets held in joint tenancy, since the surviving owner gets the deceased partner's share automatically. Particularly troubling is the possibility that your state could try and claim the total value of your house if you kept a life estate. See further in this chapter for a discussion of life estates.

The long and short of the matter is that you should be very careful in keeping an interest in assets even though you may not own or control them, because even though they may not be in your estate when you die, Medicaid could claim the entire value of the asset because you had an interest in it.

Exceptions to penalty against transferring

When you transfer your house, Medicaid disqualifies you from eligibility for benefits except in certain cases. A single person or married couple can transfer a home to:

1. a child who is blind, disabled or under 21.
2. a sibling who owns a share of the home and has resided there for at least one year before the co–holder goes into the nursing home.
3. a child (of any age) who has resided in the home for at least two years before the parent's institutionalization, and can show that he has cared for the parent at home.
4. anyone at any time, as long as it is for fair market value.

5. anyone, providing the purpose of the transfer is not to qualify for Medicaid. For example, a person gives his house to his children while healthy for the purpose of avoiding probate or estate taxes. Later, he is permanently disabled in an accident and is forced to go into a nursing home within 3 years of making the transfer. This transfer would probably not disqualify him from Medicaid.

One last possibility. Even though the transfer of a house would ordinarily disqualify a person for Medicaid, he may still receive benefits if he can show that he would suffer undue hardship by not being granted benefits. This alternative is rarely accepted by Medicaid.

Protecting a home when there is time to plan

There are only three options available to protect your home if there is time to plan. None of them is fool–proof, and it is strongly recommended that you verify the options with your local elder law attorney.

1. Give away the house
2. Give away the house with a life estate
3. Put the house in trust

1. Give away the house

A person is free to give a house to whomever he chooses and later qualify for Medicaid, providing the ineligibility period runs prior to application for Medicaid. There are three considerations before you do this.

First, giving your home away leaves you with no control. There are more than a few cases of a daughter who has tried to have parents evicted from their home, or a son who has lost the house through bad investments or a divorce.

Second, while you may trust the person or persons to whom you give your house, you sacrifice the one–time $125,000 exemption from capital gains taxes (assuming you are over 55) if you later decide to sell (see Chapter 11).

Third, by giving away your home, you pass on to the receiver a greater capital gains tax liability when the house is sold. Capital gains is the difference between the basis (what you paid for the house plus what you spent on major improvements) and the sale price. Most older Americans paid relatively little for their homes, and have seen their homes appreciate greatly in value. This low basis is passed on to the recipient of the house. When she later sells the property at fair market value, she pays a substantial tax on the capital gain (see Chapter 11).

2. Give away the house with a life estate

When a person gives away his house he may make a provision that he keep an interest in the property for the remainder of his life. That interest may take the form of a life estate through which he has a lifelong right to live in the home as well as to receive any income or benefits that may accrue from the property.

A life estate does not mean that you own the property; it means that you have an interest that ends when you die. Under new federal regulations passed on August 11, 1993, the states are required to seek reimbursement from the estate of anyone who received benefits. Many lawyers and specialists in the field believe that the new law will allow your state to place a lien on the value of your life estate upon your death. Massachusetts, for example, at one time placed a value on a life estate when a person applied for Medicaid.

Massachusetts has stopped doing it, but has indicated that it, like most states, will seek to recover money from the value of a recipient's house by placing a value on any life estate. Please check carefully with your local elder law attorney.

Even if your state places a value on a life estate, it still may be a good idea to have one, for two reasons: protecting a portion of the $125,000 exemption from capital gains given to those over 55 when they sell their house; and "stepping up" the basis on your home upon death so your heirs pay little or no capital gains tax when the property is sold.

Sit down with your accountant and go over the numbers. For example, if your dad is 85 years old and owns a house worth $150,000 for which he paid $5,000, a life estate may make sense even though Medicaid will place a lien on it upon his death for reimbursement if he needs care. The life estate may be worth only a few thousand dollars when he dies, but by keeping it, his heirs will get a new basis when they file a death tax return. If the value of the home is $150,000 at the date of his death, the new basis would be the same, which means no capital gains tax when it is sold.

One further caution. The new law regarding estate recovery is so vague, there are some experts who think keeping a life estate could subject the entire value of the house to a lien, not just the value of the life interest. Again, please check with your local elder law attorney.

3. Put the house in trust

For an explanation of trusts, please see Chapter 2. For all practical purposes, the only instrument that will protect your home at this time is an "income–only trust". You could also try an "indirect irrevocable" trust, but there is the likelihood that if you reside in your home Medicaid may say that the trust was for your benefit even though indirect.

A warning. Up until 1993, many states allowed you to place your home in a revocable trust which in turn would protect it from a Medicaid lien. The theory, correct at the time, was that welfare could only place a lien on your estate, and since the house was owned by a trust, no lien was permitted. All that has changed. It is quite possible that your state will not let you qualify for Medicaid unless your home is transferred out of the trust. That's where the problem may be; not retransferring your home, because the law allows you to do that, but rather a provision in the 1993 law that indicates that transferring the home to anyone but you could trigger a 5–year "look–back" period (see Chapter 3).

Please be careful in retransferring houses from revocable trusts.

Joint ownership: Holding your home jointly with another will at best protect only one half of it, and may mean that you lose the entire home to a lien if your state aggressively interprets 1993 federal laws. Please check with a local elder law attorney to determine how your state deals with jointly held property.

Panic — there's no time to plan

No time to plan means that a person will be going into a medical institution or nursing home and requesting Medicaid assistance within 3 years of transferring his home. Obviously, if you are facing this situation, your first concern is to protect your house.

Married couple Currently there's no problem, since the law allows the person going into the nursing home to transfer his interest to the spouse even while on Medicaid.

Single people Transferring your house within 3 years of going into a nursing home poses a difficult situation for single people. Your best option is to see if you fall into any of the exceptions mentioned in this chapter. If you don't, here's a grim option:

Don't try to transfer the house at all if it is worth a great deal of money (say, over $200,000). Medicaid will place a lien on it when you die. But since Medicaid usually pays about 75% of the private daily rate, the bite out of your estate will be less than if you pay privately for institutionalization.

For example, if a nursing home charges private pay patients $100 a day, the rate that Medicaid pays for the same person is about $75. Upon your death your family will have to pay the lien, but it's three–quarters of what the private rate would have been.

The only problem is that your state may have adopted the federal regulation that mandates that a primary residence be sold after six months of institutionalization if the patient cannot show that he will be returning home. Check with your local elder law attorney.

CHAPTER 7

LONG–TERM CARE INSURANCE

Until recently, few people understood that Medicare and all other forms of health insurance do not pay for custodial care in a nursing home. Because of recent media exposure given to the subject of catastrophic illness, more people have begun to face the seriousness of the problem. When an illness strikes that requires long-term custodial care, there are only three alternatives that will pay: cash, Medicaid and long–term care insurance.

Understand that if you want coverage for a nursing home, an assisted living facility or home care, you have to buy a long–term care policy. Medicare will pay for hospitalization and doctors bills with a deductible that is covered by so called Medigap policies.These plans will not cover long–term care.

Long–term care insurance

Long–term care insurance pays a certain dollar amount per day for a set number of months or years of skilled, intermediate, or custodial care in a nursing home. Some policies pay for this care only in a nursing home, other policies pay for care only at home. The better policies pay for nursing homes, assisted living facilities, and home health care. Home health care coverage should include home health aides, homemakers, adult day care, companion care, and respite care.

Two things are guaranteed in the field of long–term care: the cost of a nursing home bed will rise substantially, and federal and state governments will continue to tighten eligibility requirements.

The consensus among attorneys who handle Medicaid issues is that long–term care insurance is a viable alternative to divesting your life savings.

Kennedy–Kassebaum Bill

An earlier edition of this book predicted the federal government would do three things with regard to long–term care financing: tighten Medicaid eligibility, set standards for long–term care insurance, and give incentives for those persons who purchased long–term care insurance.

The Health Insurance Portability & Accountability Act of 1996, otherwise known as the Kennedy-Kassebaum Bill, addressed all three items.

Medicaid planning appears to have been criminalized, long–term care insurance was given tax clarification, and the federal government set minimum standards for "tax–qualified" long–term care insurance. In addition, individuals are now allowed to deduct long–term care expenses that were not covered by insurance.

Tax clarification of long–term care insurance means two things: up to certain limits, the premiums paid for insurance are deductible, and the benefits (up to $175 per day) would be received tax–free to the insured. Long–term care insurance premiums can now be added along with eligible medical expenses on Schedule A, and to the extent they exceed 7½% of the insured's adjusted gross income, they are deductible.

Example: Mrs. Johnston has an annual adjusted gross income of $40,000 per year. Her eligible medical expenses and insurance premiums amount to $5,000. 7½% of her adjusted gross income is $3,000, therefore any expenses over that, in this case $2,000, are deductible.

The deduction is also subject to the following limits:

Attained age at the end of the year	Premium deduction
40 or less	$200
41-50	$375
51-60	$750
61-70	$2,000
71 and above	$2,500

Many persons do not file a long form and may not qualify for this tax deduction. However, if a couple has medical expenses (possibly prescription drugs) and both have a Medicare supplement and a "tax–qualified" long–term care policy, it may be possible for them to take advantage of the medical expense deduction. Check with your tax professional before taking any tax deductions you are unsure about.

Under current interpretation of the law, only "tax–qualified" policies, those that met the federal standards, are eligible for the tax deduction. At this printing, however, it is unclear whether the benefits paid from "non–tax–qualified" policies will be tax–free or whether they will be subject to income taxation.

If you purchased a long–term care policy before January 1, 1997 and it met the regulations in your state when you bought it, you do not need to cancel it to get a "tax–qualified" policy. The Kennedy–Kassebaum Bill specifically "grandfathered" your policy to benefit from the tax benefits of "tax–qualified" plans.

Federal long–term care insurance regulation

Responding to the need for minimum standards on long–term care policies, the NAIC developed a model regulation which, among other things, establishes minimum standards upon which long–term care policies should be based. Although NAIC has no authority to make states adopt its model regulations, most states have done so to one degree or another.

The Federal Government used the 1993 NAIC model to be the benchmark for policies that are "tax–qualified" under the Kennedy–Kassebaum Bill. "Tax–qualified" long–term care insurance plans must now offer home health care, inflation protection, and non–forfeiture as optional benefits that buyers can add to their policies. These are generally available as riders.

"Tax–qualified" policies must also have certain consumer protections, assuring your purchase of a quality policy:

1. Policies must be guaranteed renewable.
2. All insurers must offer third–party lapse notification protection.
3. Post–claims underwriting, the practice of waiting until you put in a claim to check your medical records, is prohibited.
4. Policies cannot unreasonably limit or exclude benefits; such as requiring skilled services before custodial services can be paid, or requiring a hospital stay before nursing home benefits could be paid.
5. If you replace one policy with another policy, the new insurer must waive any pre–existing conditions.
6. Benefits cannot duplicate those available from Medicare.

The benefit triggers required for persons to be eligible for benefits under a "tax–qualified" policy are specified in the regulations as well. You can receive benefits when a doctor or a licensed health care practitioner says that you are unable to perform 2 of either 5 or 6 activities of daily living, "without substantial assistance from another individual". The health professional will also have to certify that your expected need will be for more than 90 days.

You can also receive benefits when you "require substantial supervision to protect such individual from threats to health and safety due to severe cognitive impairment".

In the past, some policies utilized a medical necessity trigger as a way of receiving benefits; however, regulations under Kennedy–Kassebaum specifically ban their use in "tax–qualified" long–term care policies.

Remember that most of the new federal provisions existed in quality long–term care plans available in the last four years. If you already have a long–term care policy, check with the agent that sold it to you to determine if your policy needs to be upgraded.

Although the NAIC and federal government reforms are helpful to those who are shopping for a policy, approximately 800,000 people are currently paying for old, potentially useless policies they bought before most state regulations went into effect. The regulations are not retroactive. If you purchased a policy before 1989, it's time to review your policy before you pay another dime in premiums. You should also check with the agent who sold you the policy or the insurance company who issued it to see if any upgrades are being offered.

You can call your state Division of Insurance (see Chapter 12) to find out whether your state has adopted the federal "tax–qualified" policy regulation. Ask if a summary of the regulation or the regulation itself is available, and get the names of those companies that are approved to market long–term care policies in your state. When shopping for insurance, ask the agent to give you a copy of the policy, not just the promotional brochure about the policy. If there is any point on which you are confused by the language in the policy, ask for a clarification in writing.

Using long–term care insurance as a Medicaid planning tool

Assuming a person is healthy enough to qualify for insurance and can comfortably afford the premium, long–term care insurance is primarily useful for maintaining control over your assets until you need nursing home or home health care.

This book has presented a number of ways you can protect assets in the event of a long–term nursing home stay if you have time to plan. Every option, in one form or another, involves issues of control, taxation and family.

Giving up control gives rise to a dilemma: The best time to protect your life savings is when you're healthy. However, to do it you generally have to give away your assets and relinquish control. Let's say you decide it's worth it, and strip away all your assets. But suppose you never need a nursing home; you die peacefully in your own bed twenty years later. For two decades, you live with the discomfort of not being in control of your finances. Not an easy decision to live with.

A long–term care insurance policy buys you time. It allows you to maintain control of your countable assets until you need long–term care. If you subsequently need a nursing home, you can shift assets. The look–back period can be up to 5 years (as of 1997), but the policy will step in and pay for your care up to the dollar amount you purchased.

Example: Noreen is 65 years old and widowed with two children. She has a house and $135,000 in cash and securities. She has two options to protect her assets from a nursing home: While she's still healthy, she can give away her assets in any number of ways, or set up an irrevocable trust. As mentioned, these options share one thing in common: loss of control.

Or she can buy a long–term care insurance policy.

Like most people, Noreen wants to keep her financial independence. She doesn't want to worry about what the answer might be if she goes to her kids and asks for her money. She doesn't want to worry about her kids getting sued or divorced and thereby jeopardizing the assets. In short, she wants control.

The cost for a good policy for a person in reasonably good health, at age 65, averages between $1,500 and $2,400 a year, depending on the amount of benefits you need. For example, if a nursing home in your state costs on average $40,000 a year, a $100–a–day benefit will probably be adequate. That will not be the case if nursing home care is $75,000 where you live. To some people, that's expensive, but the alternatives of giving away your assets or placing them in an irrevocable trust to protect them will cost you too, and not just in terms of loss of control. You have to consider tax consequences as well (see Chapter 11). If the assets given away have a low basis (the price paid for the asset), you give that away too, which means when your kids sell the assets they pay a substantial capital gains tax. What if your children have kids receiving or about to receive college aid? If your children receive lump sums of money, they will probably be disqualified from receiving financial aid. There are income tax considerations as well. Your children may be in a higher tax bracket than you are, which means that much more of the income earned on the assets given away goes to the government. These are just a few of the considerations you must look at when you transfer assets.

Even if you can live with the downside of giving away assets or placing them in an irrevocable trust, can you live with this: Nursing homes do not like accepting patients who are on Medicaid because the homes are paid less than for patients paying privately, and the homes have to wait for their money. Therefore, it is likely you would have to come up with at least nine months to a year of private funds to get into a first–class facility. That means the people who hold your money may have to turn around and give back a chunk of it to get you in. How much for nine months to a year? In 10 years, figure in the neighborhood of $50,000 to $75,000. Nice neighborhood.

On the other hand, let's say you are in your early 70's and pay $3,500 a year for a policy for 10 years. At first glance, this seems like a great deal of money. But wait. Do the arithmetic. Ten years of premiums at $3,500 per year is $35,000. That's a lot better than $50,000 to $75,000, and the policy all but assures you of a bed in your choice of nursing home.

Second marriages

People entering into a second marriage usually prepare for the financial consequences of marriage in a variety of ways. Prenuptial agreements may be included, and wills redrawn to ensure that each person's assets are left to his or her children. The assets that each spouse brings into a second marriage are often held separately by that spouse.

Separate trusts may have been set up to minimize probate costs and estate taxes. In all, most people that enter into second marriages prepare for distribution of their assets after death, but fail to realize that they are unprepared if an illness requiring long–term care strikes. The problem is that Medicaid does not recognize any of these planning maneuvers. All assets held by persons that are married are considered joint assets and are countable under Medicaid laws.

Example: Eleanor Harris, widowed at age 60, met and married James May, age 70. Mrs. Harris entered the marriage with $200,000 in liquid assets from the sale of her deceased husband's business and a house in Minnesota worth $225,000. She holds these assets in her name only and has a will leaving these assets to her four children equally. Mr. May entered the marriage with $120,000 in liquid assets which he also keeps in his own name and has willed to his only child. Mr. May also has a pension of $2,000 per month. Together they purchase and move into a condo in Florida.

After three years of marriage, Mr. May developed Alzheimer's disease and needed nursing home care. It took three years of nursing home care to exhaust his $120,000 in assets. Mrs. Harris thought that because her assets were held in her name only, they would be protected and that Medicaid would now pay for her husband's nursing home care.

She is shocked to learn that she is now legally responsible for the cost of his care until such time as she has spent her assets down to $79,020 (as of

1997). If her home is not their primary residence, she will have to sell that as well!

If Mr. May had purchased a long–term care policy to pay for the costs of his long–term care, Mrs. Harris's assets would remain protected for her and her children. Anyone entering into a second marriage, especially where there is a substantial difference in age, should have a long–term care policy.

Some things to look for in a long–term care policy

Length of benefits

Since Medicaid planning may fit into part of your long–term care needs, it is important that your policy pay the cost of a nursing home for at least 4 years. Medicaid requires a 36–month look–back period. If your policy pays for 3 years, you could be eligible for Medicaid once the policy ran out, assuming you made a transfer of assets prior to going into a nursing home.

Why then purchase a 4-year benefit? Many of my clients have assets, such as a house and/or stock, with a low cost basis. That means that they didn't pay much for the assets. If these assets are transferred, the person receiving them gets the low cost basis as well. When these assets are sold, there will be a substantial capital gains tax liability. If those assets are retained by my clients, and are in their estate when they die, there will be a free step–up to current market value as of the date of death. By purchasing a four–year benefit, the family has a year to determine if their loved one will survive. If the chances are not good, keep the assets in his or her name.

Since the average stay in a nursing home is seldom more than 3 years, that may be all the coverage you need. However, almost everyone has heard of someone that has been in a nursing home for a lot longer. Look at the difference in premiums for an extra year of benefits in case you were to exceed the average stay in a nursing home. If the difference in cost is not that significant and it will help you sleep better, insure for a longer benefit period.

If you are purchasing coverage in your early 50s, you will find that the difference in premiums between four years of coverage and lifetime coverage is insignificant.

Nursing home daily benefit

Before deciding on how much benefit to purchase, check to see how much the daily nursing home cost is in the area in which you live or to which you would be most likely to move in the event you needed long–term care. If family members are located out of state, you might find yourself moving to that state in the event you need a nursing home, so that you might be closer to your family.

Now decide how much of that cost you are willing to self–insure and how much you want the insurance company to pay. It makes good sense to use some of your income to pay for the costs of the nursing home and just let the insurance company pay the difference. That way you need less insurance and you keep your premiums down.

Optional inflation rider

This rider can be critical. If you don't elect to take it, your coverage will be continually eroded by the rising cost of long–term care. You will have to pay tomorrow's inflated bills with today's devalued dollars. Since most people who go into a nursing home are in their mid–eighties, the younger you are when you buy a policy, the more important inflation protection becomes. If you are buying a policy at a relatively young age in order to fix a lower rate, you may not need the benefits for many years, by which time inflation (which rises at a compounded rate) will have greatly diminished your benefits.

Unfortunately, even the most generous rider available in policies lags well behind the actual rate of increase in medical care costs. That means that the policyholder's benefits could diminish every year. If you are purchasing insurance under age 70, it would be a good idea to choose a policy that offers inflation riders that are compounded annually, rather than those that increase on a simple–interest basis. The cost of adding an inflation rider can increase the cost of a policy by as much as 40% at some ages, but it is an essential part of a good policy.

For people in their late 70s and early 80s that are buying policies, it may make more sense to purchase a policy that offers a CPI (Consumer Price Index) or a Guaranteed Purchase Option instead of a built–in inflation rider, since the cost of the built–in rider is so high. Having a CPI or GPO inflation option means that the insurance company will allow you to add benefits to your policy every 1–3 years to keep pace with rising costs without evidence of insurability.

Some companies base this increase on what the CPI was for that year, while other companies use a flat 5% or 8%. If you figure out the premiums using this approach for people in their late 70s and early 80s, you will find this method actually cheaper over the long run. If the policy you want to purchase does not offer a future guaranteed purchase option or CPI inflation protection, you may want to purchase $30–$50 per day above what is actually needed to cover any further increase in the cost of care.

Home health care

Unless a person has a strong family network that can assure a sick person that they would assist with care for as long as he or she needed it, almost everyone should make sure his or her policy has home health care benefits. Long–term illnesses are not always terminal and many people can recover from a broken hip or a stroke. The presence of home care benefits may help a person recover faster in his or her own home than in a nursing home. While Medicare does cover some limited home health care, it is entirely possible to be in a situation where the long–term care policy can pay for the charges for which Medicare will not pay. In any case, home health care benefits are much more likely to be used than nursing home benefits, and should be included in most policies.

Use a similar method for determining the home health care benefit as used for the nursing home benefit. Check with some local home health care agencies to see what the hourly rate and availability is for home health aides, homemakers, and companions, since these are the services most likely to be used.

It also may make sense to insure a higher percentage of the home care benefit needed, and depend less on your income, since when you need home care, all the other expenses associated with running your household are continuing. Always insure for at least a one– or two–year benefit period for home health care.

Assisted living facilities

The last few years have seen a major shift in thinking about how older Americans should be taken care of. Up until a few years ago, there were few, if any, facilities available to provide for a person who found it difficult to get through a daily routine, but yet was not sick enough to need nursing home care. Assisted living facilities have filled this void.

Similar to upscale hotels, they offer individuals or couple an apartment and services that allow them to maintain their independence longer. For example, there is no maintenance required; meals are prepared and served, either in the dining room or in their apartment; medical staff is available on short notice to handle problems; and facilities provide for additional help in assisting a resident through his or her daily routine. Generally, these facilities are in a campus–like setting adjacent to a nursing home. Long–term care policies will pay many of the expenses, but you should clearly understand what is and is not covered.

Deductibles or elimination periods

All long–term care policies offer deductible periods or elimination periods in their policies. These are the number of days you pay for either nursing home or home health care on your own before the insurance policy kicks in. These deductibles can range from a zero–day deductible up to a 365–day deductible. Choosing a deductible is a personal choice. Ask yourself the question: how long could you afford to pay for the cost of long–term care before the insurance company starts to pay? Since longer deductibles lower insurance premiums, make sure the agent shows you all the choices available from that particular company and weigh the savings to determine what is best for you. A longer deductible for nursing home benefits may be easier to accept than a long deductible for home health care, as most home care needs appear to be short term. Some policies offer great savings on premiums to persons who take longer deductibles, while other companies do not have a great deal of difference in premiums between deductibles.

Non–forfeiture or return–of–premium features

A question always brought up when people are considering the purchase of long–term care insurance is what happens to all the money we spent on premiums if we don't use the policy? Good question! The answer is that like every other kind of insurance you own, with the exception of certain types of life insurance, long–term care insurance premiums are paid and if you need benefits the protection is there, but if you cancel the policy there is no cash value left in the policy.

Responding to criticism that many long–term care policies lapse in the first few years they are in force, many insurance companies are now offering return–of–premium or non–forfeiture benefits. Are these riders a good idea? If paying an extra 25%–45% in premiums for your policy to get a benefit that pays only if you drop your policy at some time in the future makes sense to you, then buy it. Some non–forfeiture options state that the policy will have some paid–up benefits left in it if you stop paying the premiums after 5–10 years.

Before deciding, however, make sure that the agent shows you a chart listing the future value the policy would have under this option. While most companies now offer this option, you should not purchase long–term care insurance if you are not sure you can afford to make the payments over a long period of time, even if there is an increase in the premium at a later date. Insurance companies are allowed to raise rates for an entire class of people, even though they can't single you out for an increase. If you have to drop the policy because you can no longer afford it, without nonforfeiture benefits you will receive nothing back.

Benefit triggers

An event must take place in order for you to receive benefits from your long–term care policy. You can't be "sick of cooking" and get the insurance company to pay for a homemaker (although they could probably sell a lot of policies if they had that feature). Benefit triggers the companies use to define when benefits are paid to the insured are now similar from policy to policy. Federal regulations under Kennedy–Kassebaum state that the only two triggers allowed in "tax–qualified" plans are the inability to perform activities of daily living, and cognitive impairment.

Older policies were often criticized for using only a "medical necessity" benefit trigger, since it was felt this could exclude benefits for people who were just frail, with a disability, or suffering from Alzheimer's disease. The later generation of long–term care policies started using the term "inability to perform activities of daily living" to cover those persons with a disability and "cognitive impairment" to cover those persons with senile dementia. "Tax–qualified" plans are not allowed to have a "medical necessity" benefit trigger.

Alternate care plans

None of us has a crystal ball. We don't know what long–term care services will look like in the future, so it makes sense to have some flexibility in the policy you are buying. Better policies will include provisions for using the nursing home benefit portion of the policy for "alternative care" or through an "alternate plan of care" benefit. Although the actual wording varies from company to company, this feature allows the nursing home benefits to be used for "alternatives" to nursing home confinement, such as benefits for assisted living facilities and/or home care.

For example, a policy holder and his family are allowed to present a plan of care to the insurance company that permits the individual to stay at home and still receive benefits or provide benefits for an assisted living facility. Likewise the insurance company may offer an alternative to the family of the insured for an "alternate setting" to the one that has been chosen. Exercising your "alternate plan of care" benefit at time of claim is voluntary, and does not detract from the insurance company's contractual obligations. This type of flexibility may be very important in the future, as the graying of America may change long–term care services as we know them.

Survivorship benefits

Some insurance companies are now offering "survivorship benefits" to couples purchasing long–term care policies together. This benefit may vary from company to company, but, typically, if a policy premium has been paid for a period of time, usually 10 years, and one of the spouses dies, the surviving spouse's policy becomes "paid–up" with no further premiums required. This can be an excellent feature when there is a considerable age difference between spouses.

Informal caregiver benefit

An interesting feature being offered in some policies is the "informal caregiver benefit." An informal caregiver clause means that benefits for home health care can be paid not only for a home health aide or homemaker but also for a family member or neighbor who is assisting with a person's care. Since this benefit can easily be overutilized by a policy holder, the policies offering this type of coverage are very expensive in comparison to those policies that do not offer it. This type of coverage is especially important for people who live in very rural areas away from professional caregivers, and that depend on family and neighbors for assistance.

Employer group and group trust policies

There are two different types of group long–term care policies on the market today: employer group and group trust. Employer group policies are offered by employers to their employees, usually on a voluntary basis, and often the premiums are paid through payroll deduction. Contrary to popular belief, group policies are not always cheaper than individual policies. Since the screening or underwriting process for some employer group policies is less stringent than for individual policies, the premiums on somc group policies can be higher and the coverages can be less comprehensive than those of individual policies. There are some innovative group policies being developed that may hold some promise for solving some of the drawbacks in the long–term care area. But be very careful. Do not buy on price alone.

Group trust policies are not true groups as we think of that term; rather they are master group trusts set up in states with lenient insurance regulation. The "master group trust" then sells "group certificates" off the master trust to individuals. Some states do not regulate group trusts, so an insurance company will often set up a group trust to skirt the regulations in a state in which it wishes to sell. The insurance company now holds all the control. If a rate increase is needed by the insurance company, it can raise your premium by just sending you a notice in the mail. This differs under an individual policy, since then the insurance company must get state approval for any rate increase. An individual policy is a contract between you and the insurance company, while a group trust policy is a contract between you and the group.

Insurance companies tailor their policies to the regulations in each state. In fact, if an insurance company wants to satisfy the insurance regulators in all 50 states, they must have 28 versions of their policy to comply with all the states. Some uniformity of long–term care insurance policies has been addressed federally with the "tax–qualified" policy regulations. Therefore, these examples may not work out the same way in your state. The costs and benefits may be different, but the problems will be the same. Wherever you live, if you buy a policy without inflation protection, your coverage will effectively shrink every year. With non–compounded inflation protection it still diminishes, but not as much.

As a general rule, with long–term care insurance you get what you pay for. The best coverage can be expensive. The more affordable policies generally offer only partial protection.

Single–premium plans and life insurance with long–term care riders

Another interesting type of long–term care coverage that a handful of companies have started to sell is not long–term care insurance at all, but life insurance with long–term care insurance riders ("life insurance w/LTC rider"). The concept appears straightforward. The policy provides two types of protection: life insurance, which, of course, is guaranteed to be paid (later rather than sooner, you hope!) and long–term care coverage, should you need it.

This feature is added to the life insurance policy by way of a rider. This rider is simply a clause that allows you to use the value of the life insurance to pay for long–term care services.

The biggest advantage to this type of contract is that by paying for the life insurance, you've also paid for the long–term care coverage. You access the long–term care coverage by drawing down on the death benefit. How much of the total benefit you can use depends upon the insurance carrier, but it is usually a percentage of the death benefit per month (typically 2%-4%).

The life insurance also builds cash value: should you discontinue the coverage, you'll see something for the years you invested your premium dollars. This type of policy can be very attractive to those individuals who don't like the idea of investing in a product such as long–term care insurance which they may never use. One way or the other, you will receive a benefit for dollars spent.

The focus of this chapter, however, is on long–term care benefits. What you get in the form of coverage is either a percentage of the face amount of the life insurance benefit, or a flat amount of coverage which you choose when you first enroll in the policy.

Example: George, age 60, is interested in purchasing a single–premium life insurance policy with a face value (a death benefit) of $75,000. The policy offers a long–term care rider.

Let's look at the policy more closely. The single–premium feature means that no additional monies will be owed to keep the policy in force. In the trade it's referred to as a "paid–up" policy. When George dies, the policy will pay his beneficiary $75,000. Typically, the single premium for this amount of insurance would be approximately $30,000. However, the actual amount varies depending upon your age and your health.

There is an immediate and continuing cash surrender value if you decide to cash in the policy. Of course, how much you actually get back depends on how long you keep it. In effect, the policy offered to George is no different from the thousands of paid–up insurance contracts offered every day.

However, George's insurance company has chosen to offer additional benefits by allowing him to draw down on the $75,000 death benefit to pay for long–term care if needed. This is the rider provision of the contract. As mentioned above, the company will pay a daily benefit which is a percentage of the total death benefit (in this case, $75,000).

The company George used, like most, will not pay more than 4% of the death benefit per month. Therefore the maximum George could receive in benefits for long–term care is $3,000 per month.

The terms and conditions of how the policy is used to pay for long–term care are similar to those of stand–alone long–term care contracts, but in some cases could be more restrictive.

There are several other differences in these two types of policies, but they tend towards personal preference rather than substance. For example, while both types of policies offer home health care, many stand–alone long–term care policies also offer custodial home care, which may include chore services and personal care attendants; most life insurance policies with long–term care riders do not. However there is one major difference which must be noted: inflation protection.

Inflation protection: Life insurance with long–term care rider

Since the daily benefit is usually based on a percentage of the death benefit, your benefits do not rise unless your death benefit does. However, most life insurance policies with long–term care riders have face amounts that are fixed and do not increase, therefore your daily benefit doesn't.

Inflation protection: Stand–alone long–term care insurance

First, you have to remember that policies of this type offer inflation protection only as an option. Typically, the daily benefit will increase by 5% per year, which can be either simple or compounded.

As with any product, there are bound to be variations. Here is one of them:

Betty, age 60, purchases a single premium policy. The amount of the single premium she paid is $75,000. This insurance company automatically doubles the death benefit to $150,000. Therefore, the amount of long–term care coverage is also doubled to $150,000.

Here's an interesting aside. Let's say you like the idea of life insurance with a long–term care rider. Your family might like it also, but for the wrong reason. Might they not consider skimping on your care if you need a nursing home, to preserve the death benefit? Hmm!

You also need to consider that under current tax treatment any benefits paid to you would be taxed just like any withdrawal of a life insurance policy.

The concept of life insurance with a long–term care rider may be especially attractive to persons in their late forties and early fifties who need life insurance and recognize the eventual need for long–term care, but may view the purchase of stand–alone coverage as too premature.

Post–claims underwriting

In October 1989, *Consumer Reports* printed an article entitled "Paying for a nursing home", which spotlighted another problem that was being scrutinized by the National Association of Insurance Commissioners — the practice of "post–claims underwriting." At the time, many insurance companies made a practice of waiting until you made a claim to determine your fitness for coverage — and it was legal. What this meant was: You might have put in a claim as much as two years after you began paying for your policy and be told, "Sorry, you're not eligible because you didn't disclose that condition when we sold you the policy." The condition might have occurred some years ago — before the period you were asked to disclose.

Nevertheless, you could still be ineligible. Or, your claim might be refused if you told the agent who sold you the policy about the condition and he or she neglected to write it down, or if you didn't tell the agent about the condition. While the practice of post–claims underwriting is now prohibited, the safest way around any problems at time of claim is when the insurance company actually requests from your doctor your medical records to determine your eligibility for a policy. If you have two or more serious conditions, it might be wise to have the agent attach a copy of your medical records with the application. When you receive the policy, check the copy of your actual application to the insurance company, which is in the last pages of your policy, for any information that the agent might have left out.

One way to be absolutely certain that future claims will not be a problem is to be thorough and honest in answering all questions on the application. Don't even think about hiding any medical problem, big or small. Double–check the application after the agent fills it out, to be sure there are no errors or omissions. Any of these might later be used by the company to rescind your coverage.

It is probably a good idea to see if the insurance company releases any information about their records on claims, or to see whether the agent has some experiences with the company he or she is representing with regard to claims.

A lot has changed since the early introduction of long–term care polices. Many states have adopted guidelines established by the Kennedy–Kassebaum legislation. Some have enacted special training requirements for agents who want to sell long–term care insurance.

Despite all the past problems, long–term care insurance is now a terrific idea because it allows you maximum control of your financial destiny. This type of insurance is useful primarily for people with substantial assets to protect, enough discretionary income to cover the premiums easily, and anxiety about the possibility of institutionalization.

Perhaps the greatest advantage of personally financing long–term care through a long–term care policy is the freedom of choice gained. How, when, and where long–term care is provided is totally under the control of the care recipient and his or her doctor when long–term care insurance is involved. The existence of home health care benefits in a long–term care policy may even be enough, along with family assistance, to keep an elderly person out of a nursing home.

When you are considering purchasing a policy, you must weigh all the factors that are specific to your own situation. An insurance agent is not an unbiased resource in helping you make a decision. If you are on a tight budget, it's probably not for you, or you might enlist family members in assisting you to pay the premium; after all, it's their inheritance you are protecting.

If you decide that long–term care insurance is a good option for you, don't buy until you thoroughly educate yourself. Some tips: Think twice before choosing a policy from anything less than an "A"–rated company. Send for the NAIC booklet *A Shopper's Guide to Long–Term Care* (see Resources).

When should you buy long–term care insurance

The answer is: at the first moment you become concerned over the cost of possible future long–term care and you decide that Medicaid is not for you. Why? Because every day after that, long–term care insurance will become more expensive for you because of your age, and it might become unavailable to you because of changing health. Ideally, people would buy fairly rich benefit policies very inexpensively when they are in their 50s. Unfortunately, most people in their 50s are not thinking about long–term care and nursing homes.

Some people think that the longer they wait to purchase long–term care insurance, the fewer years they'll have to pay premiums, and therefore it would cost them less in the long run. Insurance companies are a lot smarter than that. The last thing they would do is to price their policies to give you the incentive to wait before buying. No way! Even taking into account the amount of years you will pay for the policy, the cumulative premiums paid over your lifetime will be lower the younger you are when you take out the coverage.

Robert Wood Johnson Foundation Partnership Plans

Although this program is available on a limited basis in only 11 states, it merits discussion since it is an interesting idea of a way to protect assets and reduce the Medicaid budgets for states. Since 1991, 11 states were able to obtain Medicaid waivers from the Health Care Financing Administration and offer asset protection from Medicaid if the person had purchased a special state–certified long–term care policy. It works a little differently in each state, but the two main premises are:

1. The Dollar–for–Dollar approach. Connecticut was the first state to offer a Partnership Plan. By purchasing a Partnership–certified policy, a policyholder receives from Medicaid a dollar of

protection of his or her own assets for every dollar the insurance company spends in the insured's care.

For instance: Mr. Johnson has a total of $100,000 in assets. He purchases a state–certified long–term care insurance policy with a total maximum payout value of $100,000. Should Mr. Johnson need long–term care, the insurance company would pay out the daily benefit, and when the policy finishes paying all the benefits, Mr. Johnson goes on Medicaid and he gets to keep his $100,000 in assets. His income would continue to go towards his nursing home bill.

2. Complete Asset Approach. In New York state, all a person needs to purchase is a Partnership–certified policy that pays for at least three years of nursing home at a minimum of $100 per day or six years of home health care at $50 per day or a combination of both. Once a person's policy runs out of benefits, that person becomes eligible for Medicaid and all of his or her assets are protected. As is the case with Connecticut, all of the person's income above

what the spouse at home is allowed to keep must continue to go to the nursing home.

Unfortunately, the passage of OBRA '93 eliminated any future Medicaid waivers to states wanting to implement similar plans.

Outlook from Washington

1996 will go down in history as the year Congress and President Clinton enacted legislation that seriously impacted the way this country will finance long–term care. Medicaid planning through trusts and transfers has been seriously limited, even criminalized in some cases.

Tax incentives and clarification have been given to long–term care insurance. What's next? Probably even more stringent Medicaid regulations, and even greater incentives for those who insure their own long–term care.

CHAPTER 8

NEGOTIATING WITH A NURSING HOME

The single most difficult decision many people ever make is to put a parent or spouse into a nursing home. The decision always feels wrong. When the choice becomes unavoidable, it is made with guilt, sadness, and a sense of failure.

At such a time, you are emotionally unprepared to negotiate with a nursing home. Rather than shopping around to find the fairest price and researching the best services, the most you may be able to handle is one simple question: "Do you have a bed for my father?"

It's difficult enough to cope with the illness, let alone to investigate nursing homes. This chapter can't make the decision any less painful for you but it can help you understand how nursing homes operate and give you some tools to help you plan.

The nursing home's agenda

You are in a better position to evaluate nursing homes if you understand something about how their finances operate. Nursing homes generally are paid by three sources: cash, Medicaid and long–term care insurance. By far, the two most common forms of payment are cash and Medicaid. In most states, well over 70% of the nursing home population is on Medicaid.

With few exceptions, the rate for private pay patients is much higher than Medicaid's rate. Nursing homes are reimbursed by Medicaid through a complex formula based on several factors, such as the age of the facility, level of care, location, and capital improvements. Medicaid builds a small profit into the rate it pays nursing homes. Their real profits come from those who pay privately.

Though the demand for beds exceeds the supply, nursing homes are not making the killing that many people think they are. Their costs for labor are high, especially in urban areas. Capital improvements to bring the facilities up to code are expensive. Any unanticipated problems, such as a delay in Medicaid reimbursement, can make the difference between survival and bankruptcy.

That's why there has been a major shake–out in the nursing home industry in recent years. Small independent operators, usually undercapitalized, have been forced to sell out to the large national chains. But even the large corporations find it difficult to make a go of it, especially in states which, because of their own money problems, do not reimburse promptly.

A perfect example is Massachusetts. In 1989, the legislature was forced to raise the income tax rate 15 percent to pay off an estimated $800 million in back Medicaid costs. Some bills to nursing homes were outstanding for as long as eight years!

Because of financial pressures, nursing homes try to avoid taking Medicaid applicants. The problem is so acute that every state and the federal government has a book full of rules prohibiting discrimination against Medicaid applicants.

Your agenda

The rest of this chapter is useless to you unless you understand that you have to spend money to secure a bed in a good nursing home, even money that could be protected by following the steps we have covered in this book. In the real world, you have to buy your way into a nursing home. Average cost of the ticket: six to nine months private pay.

Here's how to find and get a bed in a good nursing home:

At least three to four months before an anticipated nursing home placement, begin researching your options. The factors to consider when evaluating a facility are: location, level of carc provided, quality and cost.

Location

No decision about location should be made until all members of the family have been consulted. Which relatives will be visiting most often? Is there access to transportation? How close are other medical facilities such as hospitals?

Level of Care provided

The ill person should be evaluated by the appropriate state or local authorities to determine the level of care required. Usually, the higher the level number, the less care necessary. A level III patient is generally able to look after himself with moderate assistance. A level II patient is generally bedridden and in need of constant custodial care. A level I patient requires continuing medical attention.

If the patient is going in on a private–pay basis at a more independent level of care (such as level III), make absolutely certain that the facility also takes at least level II patients. Some nursing homes, upon finding out that there are no more private funds, suddenly reclassify patients. If the facility does not provide the level of care needed, they can legitimately dump the patient.

Even though this may be wrong, the last thing you want is to get into an argument.

Quality of Care

The best way to find a good nursing home is to check with your local Council on Aging, state department of elderly affairs (if any), private groups such as Alzheimer's and Parkinson's support organizations, or a hospital social worker.

Costs

You should be the one to interview the nursing home about money, not the other way around. Find out what the costs are and the price of extras such as laundry, doctors' visits, and medications. Make sure that the facility is Medicaid certified. Find out what the policy is on when payment is due. Most states do not allow a nursing home to ask for a lump sum up front. If the subject comes up, don't make a speech about it, just suggest that the state may not allow it. (The objective is to find a bed for a person who desperately needs care, not start a lawsuit.)

Keep in mind that the nursing home would rather take a private–pay patient. A commitment for a certain number of months of private pay will usually secure a bed.

LEGAL INSTRUMENTS

This chapter shows you how assets can be handled if you know that at some time in the future you will not be able to manage your own financial affairs. It is also for people who are making arrangements for friends or relatives who cannot presently handle their financial affairs.

The power of attorney — regular and durable

A power of attorney is a legal instrument that gives to another or others the right to handle financial affairs. Typically, a person will create a power of attorney to give another the right to have access to a bank account or to sell stock on his behalf. The person given this responsibility does not have to be an attorney.

A **regular power of attorney** usually gives specific and limited powers like the ones mentioned above. It usually does not have an expiration date but ceases the minute you become incapacitated.

A **durable power of attorney** is exactly the same except that it remains valid even if you become incapacitated. It can be very effective in planning to protect assets which otherwise would have to be spent on a nursing home.

Example: Peter is a widower with two children. He has $50,000 in cash and $10,000 in stock in his name only. His wife recently died in a nursing home. He is concerned about protecting his assets if he needs long–term care, but does not want to give up control while he is still healthy.

Peter could simply put his children's names on his assets. However, if one of his children gets divorced or gets into financial trouble, his assets could be in jeopardy.

Or he could make up a durable power of attorney giving authority to one or both offspring to get at his assets should he become incapacitated. If he became ill and couldn't get at his assets, let alone manage them, his children could use the power of attorney to close out the accounts and transfer the assets to their names.

Warning: Giving a power of attorney is giving away control. It is not advisable to do this unless absolutely necessary. It is best to give it to someone who is trustworthy to hold until it is needed. Instructions should be given about how and when it will be used.

If your state allows it, consider putting two people on the power of attorney so there are checks and balances.

Consider a "springing" durable power of attorney. This instrument is valid only when you become incapacitated, unlike a regular or durable power of attorney which becomes effective the moment you sign.

Make sure you update! The biggest mistake lawyers and financial advisors make when recommending powers of attorney is to forget to inform their clients that most financial institutions will not accept them after a period of time. There is no set policy on when the instrument becomes "stale." Remember, a power of attorney is only as good as a person's or institution's willingness to accept it. Update by rewriting it (if only by changing the effective date) at least every two years.

Conservatorships

A conservatorship usually means that a person has requested of an appropriate court permission to handle the assets and affairs of someone who is incapacitated (the ward). Anyone can be named a conservator. In some states the ward can participate in choosing a conservator.

Once a person is appointed by the court, she becomes responsible for handling the assets in approximately the same way the ward would. Conservatorships are almost useless in protecting assets unless the ward has at least 30 months to plan to protect countable assets.

A durable power of attorney would be just as effective as a conservatorship at a fraction of the cost and without having the court and the world know your business.

Conservatorships are most effective when a person becomes so ill that long–term management of his/her assets is necessary. Readers of this book who have acted on what they learned should not find this alternative attractive or necessary.

Those with relatives who are already ill and who may need a nursing home down the road may think that a conservatorship is the answer. The problem is that Medicaid planning, in practice, means taking the assets out of the ward's name. A conservatorship, by definition, means keeping the assets in the ward's name but under the legal control of the conservator.

Therefore, a conservator never gets assets away from Medicaid, but rather preserves them for Medicaid

Conservatorships therefore should not be considered until you consult with an attorney who understands Medicaid.

Guardianships

A guardianship is the same as a conservatorship except that the court grants to the guardian control of the ward's body as well as his assets. The guardian requests that the court grant power to make decisions about such things as medication, treatment, and even matters of life and death.

On the subject of protecting assets, it is enough to say that a guardianship has the same advantages (not many) and disadvantages (many) as a conservatorship.

CHOOSING A LAWYER

Where to look for a lawyer

The practice of Medicaid law is a very specialized field. Few lawyers can speak its language fluently.

Here are some suggestions for finding an attorney with expertise in this field:

- Call your local Council on Aging or its equivalent for referrals.
- Speak to the social worker at your area hospital. Many have dealt with nursing home placement and are familiar with attorneys who work in the field.
- Speak to your doctor, but make sure he has worked on *Medicaid* issues with the attorney he recommends.
- An excellent source of experienced attorneys is local support groups like Alzheimer's, Parkinson's and stroke victims' organizations.
- If you have a family lawyer whom you trust, ask him to find a lawyer who concentrates in the elder law field.

- If you still can't get a name of a reputable elder law attorney, see Chapter 12 for how to send away for names in your state.

Here are some suggestions on how not to find an attorney:

- Don't choose an attorney from an advertisement. Anyone can call himself an expert.
- Don't rely on your local bar association referral service. Few, if any, have a category that deals with this subject. If they deal with it at all, they lump the subject with estate planning. Estate planners do not necessarily understand Medicaid.

Interviewing a lawyer

Here are some points to raise with the attorney you are considering:

- What percentage of his practice is devoted to Medicaid law?
- Have him show you the specific regulations that cover Medicaid eligibility in your state. You'd be surprised how many lawyers don't have them.

- Ask if he has spoken or written on the subject.
- Ask him how he charges and specifically what work is performed. Make sure the attorney is willing to write you a comprehensive follow–up letter after your initial meeting. It is difficult to absorb everything the lawyer says in a first meeting. The letter will clarify questions raised and will give you the maximum benefit from this book.

Here are some telling questions for interviewing lawyers:

"I'm a little confused about how the ineligibility period works in this state."

Any lawyer who hesitates or asks you what you mean doesn't belong in this field.

"My mother is concerned that she'll lose her house if she goes into a nursing home. She wants to 'sell' it to me and and take a note from me for the purchase price. Is this a good idea?"

Basic Medicaid law dictates that you never take a non–countable asset, like a house, and convert it into a countable one, like money. Aside from the fact that you're creating an instant capital gains tax problem, the note that your mother holds could remain a countable asset for years.

"My father is becoming forgetful although he still mostly manages on his own. He has a house and $50,000. I'm concerned he may need a nursing home some day. Should I get a conservatorship?"

If the lawyer answers yes, get up and walk out. Conservators cannot shift assets without a court's permission. The conservator's job is to preserve assets. Can you imagine going to a judge and saying that you want to protect your father's assets by transferring them to yourself? Right!

The better answer from a lawyer is to suggest that you sit down with your father and explain that assets might be lost to a nursing home if he doesn't do some planning now and suggest that he take steps while he's well, such as shifting assets or setting up an irrevocable trust.

Mark up this book and take it with you when you go to see the attorney. That's what the wide margins are for. By now you have some idea of what needs to be done. Be prepared with a list of your own questions. Does the lawyer seem to know what he or she is talking about? You now have enough information to be a pretty good judge of a lawyer's expertise. If the answers you get make you uncomfortable, politely excuse yourself and find someone who knows more about the field of elder law.

TAX CONSIDERATIONS

Any plan to protect assets from the cost of catastrophic illness generally involves taking assets out of your name. That can end up being a two–edged sword: you may protect assets from a nursing home only to make them available to the federal or state government because of poor tax planning. This chapter sets forth a summary of current tax law as it applies to asset transfers. It is not intended as the final word on tax strategy — that is left to your financial advisor.

In order to take into consideration the effect of taxes on your plan, you need to be familiar with certain terms and concepts. Here they are:

Once–in–a–lifetime exemption from capital gains tax

Section 121 of the Internal Revenue Code allows homeowners who are 55 or older, and who meet certain ownership and residence requirements, to exclude from taxation up to a maximum of $125,000 of gain (net profit) from the sale of their principal residence.

To qualify, only one of the parties needs to be 55 and the home must be used as a principal residence for three out of the five years prior to the sale. If a homeowner resides in a nursing home or long–term care facility, the residency requirement is reduced to one year.

Stepped–up basis

The world of capital gains tax revolves around two points: what you paid for something and what you get when you sell it. What you paid for an asset is called a basis. The basis can be increased in many instances by adding in the cost of major improvements. For instance, if you paid $20,000 for your house and sold it for $100,000 (net the expenses in selling it) the capital gain is $80,000. If you had spent $10,000 for a new roof and kitchen, your basis would be $30,000 or a $70,000 gain when you sell. You pay taxes on the gain.

If assets are in your name when you die, their basis increases (gets "stepped–up") to the fair market value if a death tax return is filed. Assuming your children inherit the assets and sell them immediately, they will incur no capital gains tax.

Example: Roy Parker has a house currently worth $100,000 and stock worth $50,000. He paid $10,000 for the house and $5,000 for the stock. If he sells *everything during his life, he will have a capital gain of $135,000. If he dies with the assets in his name, assuming his offspring fills out a death tax return, the basis of $15,000 gets "stepped up" to the values placed on the return. If that figure is $150,000 and the offspring immediately sells it, there will be no capital gains.*

Rollover of taxable gains

Under section 1034 of the Internal Revenue Code, if you sell your home and reinvest any gain you receive in a house of equal or greater value within two years, you do not have to pay taxes on your gain. This is called a "rollover", and it allows you to trade up to a better house any number of times without incurring capital gains tax at each sale. If you buy a less expensive house, you would have to pay tax on whatever portion of your gain you do not reinvest.

Transfer of assets

1. To a spouse

There are no tax consequences on transfers between spouses. Section 1041 of the Internal Revenue Code provides that there is no taxable gain to either party unless the person receiving the property is a non–resident alien. There is also no tax consequence if transfers are made as part of a divorce settlement. The basis of the property transferred remains the same.

2. To children

Transfers to a child have the same tax consequences as transfers between spouses with two important exceptions: The total joint assets of the parents making the transfers must be under $1.2 million ($600,000 if one parent), and the child picks up the parents' basis.

Outright gifts/transfers

There is a great deal of confusion about the issue of federal gift tax. Many people think that they can only give away (transfer) up to $10,000 a year per person, ($20,000 per couple) without having to pay a gift tax.

That's only partially accurate. True, gifts under $10,000 a year are not subject to gift tax. Yearly gifts over $10,000 per person are subject to taxes but the government gives you a credit against them. The maximum credit is $192,800 which represents the tax on a gift of $600,000. Double both of those figures for a couple. This same credit is also available to be used to offset taxes on your estate when you die. That's why it's called the "unified credit against gift and death tax." A person dying with assets of $600,000 or less would incur a tax but it would be offset by the credit. If your estate is over $600,000 you might want to give away some of your assets now so all of the credit would be available to be used against your death tax. That's why people with assets over $600,000 ($1.2 million per couple) give away gifts of less that $10,000 annually. If your assets are under $600,000, you can give away as much as you want in a singe year. It doesn't really matter since the tax on both your gifts and what's left in your estate when you die will always be less than your credit.

Tax considerations in establishing:

1. An irrevocable trust

An irrevocable trust is similar to a revocable trust in that the purpose of both is to hold assets. The difference is that the person (donor) who establishes the irrevocable trust gives up control and ownership completely. In a revocable trust, although ownership is given up, full control is maintained, meaning that the donor has the power to modify or terminate the trust at any time.

Irrevocable trusts are taxed as separate taxpayers on any income not distributed to beneficiaries during the year. Great care must be taken if this type of trust is to be used since it is likely that all income, gain, loss, deductions and credits would apply only to the trust and not to the individual. If, for example, you place your primary residence in an irrevocable trust and it was later sold, you would not, in most cases, be able to claim the once–in–a–lifetime $125,000 exemption from capital gains tax.

2. A revocable trust

These are also referred to as "grantor" or "donor" trusts. Since the person establishing them maintains the right to terminate or modify them, these instruments do not exist for tax purposes. Therefore, any income, loss, gain, deduction or credit would stay with the person who established the trust.

3. A life estate

A life estate is an outright transfer of a person's home or other real estate with one provision: The persons transferring the property, typically parents, reserve the right to live in the property for their lifetimes, collect any rental income, pay taxes and take deductions. In short, they have a "life interest" in that property. Best of all, the property avoids a Medicaid lien.

The children, although they have ownership, cannot sell, mortgage, rent, or evict the life tenant.

These are the the tax benefits:

1. The parent(s) can deduct expenses and claim any income on their tax return. The children have no tax obligation.
2. The property goes through their taxable estate upon the parents' deaths, which means the basis gets "stepped up" (see above).

These are the tax disadvantages:

1. Elderly people often qualify for an abatement (decrease) of their real estate taxes. Any abatement of real estate taxes is lost.
2. The person transferring the property reduces the once–in–a–lifetime $125,000 exemption from capital gains tax to the value of the life estate.

3. The property no longer qualifies for rollover treatment under Section 1034 of the Internal Revenue Code.
4. The property may be vulnerable to lawsuits brought against the children who now own it or be subject to being divided if a child gets divorced.

Deductibility of nursing home expenses

Many people enter a nursing home as private–pay patients. Although they may not be eligible for Medicaid, they may be able to save on their income taxes by deducting their medical expenses. In order to qualify as a legitimate deduction under Internal Revenue Code 213, expenses for medical care must exceed 7.5 percent of the taxpayer's adjusted gross income.

If a physician states that a primary reason for institutionalization was the need for medical care, then all nursing home expenses, not just the medical portion are deductible. If a person is in a nursing home for custodial care, rather than strictly medical care, he may not be able to deduct the cost of his meals and lodging but could deduct whatever expenses were medical in nature.

When taking tax deductions for medical expenses, you need to keep good records of all expenses. These may include statements from doctors, bills for treatments, medications, transportation, eyeglasses and hearing aids, medical insurance premiums, etc.

Dependency exemption

If an institutionalized person has transferred assets to a child, the child may find it necessary to pay the nursing home bill for a period of time. Often the child can claim a dependency exemption for the parent (or grandparent, for that matter). Or, if there are several relatives helping out with expenses, the exemption and deductions can be allocated among them.

In order to qualify as a dependent, a person must receive less than $2,000 of gross income per taxable year and meet the following criteria which the IRS uses to define a dependent:

1. Over half of the dependent's support for the year was provided by the person claiming the exemption

2. The dependent is a U.S. citizen
3. The dependent did not file a joint return
4. The dependent is related to the taxpayer

Questionnaire 1

What is the minimum and maximum amount of assets the spouse not going into the nursing home (community spouse) may keep?

To find out how many countable assets (see Chapter 2) such as cash a community spouse may keep, use the following hypothetical question when contacting your local Department of Public Welfare. For a listing of the Department in your state, please see Resources, Chapter 13.

Question 1

"My spouse is going to need nursing home care. We have $100,000 in cash and other non-exempt assets. What is the minimum amount of assets I will be allowed to keep?"

Answer:

Question 2

"What is the maximum amount of assets I can keep?"

Answer:

Typically, there can be only one of two answers, because the federal government has established a minimum and a maximum amount. In 1997, the minimum was $15,804 and the maximum —

$79,020.However, the federal government has allowed the states to raise the floor. For example, New York and Florida have raised the floor to $79,020 in 1997. Therefore the answer to question 1 could be anywhere from $15,804 to $79,020. The ceiling may be raised only by the federal government.

Questionnaire 2

What may I keep as non–countable (also called exempt) assets?

The following is a list of questions that you should ask your local Department of Public Welfare. For a listing of your local office, please see Resources, Chapter 13.

Question 1

"How much cash may a person keep once he or she has qualified for Medicaid?"

Answer:

Question 2

"May a person spend an unlimited amount on a funeral so long as it is prepaid?"

Answer:

"If not, what is the maximum amount?"

Answer:

Question 3

"How much can a person requesting Medicaid spend on a car?"

Answer:

Question 4

"Please tell me what the policy is on keeping a house if it is a primary residence. Specifically I want to know:

Will you place a lien on the house? If yes, when?

Answer:

Will you force the house to be sold while my (father, aunt, husband, etc.) is on Medicaid? If yes, please tell me when and how?

Answer:

May my (father, aunt, husband etc.) prevent the house from being sold by stating he intends to return home?

Answer:

What type of life insurance may my (father, aunt, spouse etc.) keep?"

Answer:

Question 5

"My (father, aunt, spouse etc.) owns a business which he/she relies on for a living. Is he /she allowed to keep it?"

Answer:

Questionnaire 3

Does my state place a limit on the amount of income I may have to qualify for Medicaid?

Many states limit access to Medicaid benefits by setting a monthly limit on the amount of income an individual may have. These are referred to as "cap states". For a complete explanation, please see Chapter 5.

To determine if your state caps monthly income, use the following questions when talking to your local Department of Public Welfare. For a complete listing of welfare offices, please see Resources, Chapter 13.

Question 1

"Will Medicaid pay for nursing home care as long as my (father, uncle, spouse etc.) has monthly income that it less than the monthly nursing home bill?"

Answer:

If the answer is yes, you are not in a "cap state". If the answer is no, then ask:

"What is the monthly limit on the income he may have?"

Answer:

If you live in a "cap state", please read Chapter 5.

State Medicaid offices

ALABAMA
Alabama Medicaid Agency
2500 Fairlane Drive
Montgomery AL 36130
(205) 277-2710

ALASKA
Division of Medical Assistance
Dept of Health & Social Services
P.O. Box H
Juneau, AK 99811
(907) 465-3355

ARIZONA
Arizona Health Care Cost
Containment System (AHCCS)
801 East Jefferson
Phoenix, AZ 85034
(602) 244-3655

ARKANSAS
Arkansas Dept of Human
Resources
Medicaid
P.O. Box 1437
Little Rock, AR 72203
(501) 682-8502

CALIFORNIA
Medical Care Services
Dept of Health Services
714 P Street, Room 1253
Sacramento,CA 95814
(916) 332-5824

COLORADO
Colorado Dept of Social Services
Health & Medical Services
1575 Sherman Street, 10th Floor
Denver, CO 80203
(303) 866-5901

CONNECTICUT
Dept of Income Maintenance
110 Bartholomew Avenue
Hartford, CT 06106
(203) 566-2008

DELAWARE
Division of Social Services
Dept of Health & Social Services
Medicaid
P.O. Box 906
1901 N. Dupont Highway
Briggs Building
New Castle, DE 19720
(302) 421-6140

DISTRICT OF COLUMBIA
Office of Health Care Financing
DC Dept of Human Services
2100 Martin Luther King, Jr
Avenue SE
Suite 302
Washington, DC 20020
(202) 727-0735

FLORIDA
Medicaid Provider/Consumer
Relations
1317 Winewood Boulevard
Building 6, Room 260
Tallahassee, FL 32399
(904) 488-8291

GEORGIA
Georgia Dept of Medical
Assistance
2 Martin Luther King, Jr Drive
1220-C West Tower
Atlanta, GA 30334
(404) 656-4479

HAWAII
Health Care Administration
Dept of Human Services
P.O. Box 339
Honolulu, Hl 96809
(808) 586 5392

IDAHO
Bureau of Welfare Medical
Programs
Dept of Health & Welfare
450 W. State Street
Boise, ID 83720
(208) 334-5747

ILLINOIS
Division of Medical Programs
Illinois Dept of Public Aid
201 S. Grand Avenue East
Springfield, IL 62743
(217) 782-2570

INDIANA
Indiana State Dept of Public Welfare
100 N. Senate Avenue
State Office Building, Rm 701
Indianapolis, IN 46204
(317) 232-6865

IOWA
Division of Medical Services
Dept of Human Services
Hoover State Office Building
Des Moines, IA 50319
(515) 281-8621

KANSAS
Dept of Social & Rehabilitative Services
Division of Medical Services
1915 Harrison Street
Docking State Office Building
Room 628-S
Topeka, KS 66612
(913) 296-3981

KENTUCKY
Dept of Medicaid Services
275 E. Main Street, 3rd Floor
Frankfort, KY 40621
(502) 564-4321

LOUISIANA
Bureau of Health Services Financing
P.O. Box 91031
Baton Rouge, LA 70821
(504) 342-3956

MAINE
Dept of Human Services
Bureau of Income Maintenance
State House Station #11
Whitten Road
Augusta, ME 04333
(207) 289-5088

MARYLAND
Medical Care Policy Administration
201 W. Preston Street
Baltimore, MD 21201
(301) 225-1432

MASSACHUSETTS
Division of Medical Assistance
650 Washington Street
Boston, MA 02111
(617) 348-5500

MICHIGAN
Medical Services Administration
Dept of Social Services
P.O. Box 30037
Lansing, Ml 48909
(517) 335-5000

MINNESOTA
Dept of Human Services
Health Care Programs Division
444 Lafayette Road
St. Paul, MN 55155
(612) 296-8517

MISSISSIPPI
Division of Medicaid
801 Robert E. Lee Building
239 N. Lamar Street
Jackson, MS 39201
(601) 359-6050

MISSOURI
Division of Medical Services
Dept of Social Services
P.O. Box 6500
Jefferson City, MO 65102
(314) 751-3425

MONTANA
Medicaid Services Division
Dept of Social & Rehabilitation Services
111 Sanders Street
P.O. Box 4210
Helena, MT 59604
(406) 444-4540

NEBRASKA
Nebraska Dept of Social Services
301 Centennial Mall South
P.O. Box 95026
Lincoln, NE 68509
(402) 471-3121

NEVADA
Division of Welfare
Dept of Human Resources
2527 N. Carson Street
Carson City, NV 89710
(702) 687-4378

NEW HAMPSHIRE
Division of Human Services
Office of Medical Services
6 Hazen Drive
Concord, NH 03301
(603) 271-4344

NEW JERSEY
Division of Medical Assistance & Health Services
Dept of Human Services
CN-712
7 Quakerbridge Plaza
Trenton, NJ 08625
(609) 588-2600

NEW MEXICO
Medical Assistance Division
Dept of Human Services
P.O. Box 2348
Santa Fe, NM 87504
(505) 827-4315

NEW YORK
Division of Medical Assistance
New York State Dept of Social Services
40 N. Pearl Street
Albany, NY 12243
(518) 474-9132

NORTH CAROLINA
Division of Medical Assistance
Dept of Human Resources
1985 Umstead Drive
P.O. Box 29529
Raleigh, NC 27626
(919) 733-2060

NORTH DAKOTA
North Dakota Dept of Human Services
Medical Services
600 East Boulevard
Bismark, ND 58505
(701) 224-2321

NORTHERN MARIANA ISLANDS
Dept of Community & Cultural Affairs
Office of the Governor
Saipan, CM 96950
(670) 332-9722

OHIO
Dept of Human Services
Medicaid Administration
30 E. Broad Street, 31st Floor
Columbus, OH 43266
(614) 644-0140

OKLAHOMA
Division of Medical Services
Dept of Human Services
P.O. Box 25352
Oklahoma City, OK 73125
(405) 557-2539

OREGON
Office of Medical Assistance
Dept of Human Resources
203 Public Service Building
Salem, OR 97310
(503) 378-2263

PENNSYLVANIA
Dept of Public Welfare
Health & Welfare Building
P.O. Box 2675
Harrisburg, PA 17120
(717) 787-3119

RHODE ISLAND
Dept of Human Services
600 New London Avenue
Cranston, RI 02920
(401) 464-3575

PUERTO RICO
Dept of Social Services
P.O. Box 11398
Santurce, PR 00910
(809) 722-7400

SOUTH CAROLINA
South Carolina Health & Human Services Finance Commission
1801 Main Street
Columbia, SC 29201
(803) 253-6128

SOUTH DAKOTA
Medical Services
Dept of Social Services
700 Governor's Drive
Kneip Building
Pierre, SD 57501
(605) 773-3495

TENNESSEE
Bureau of Medicaid
729 Church Street
Nashville, TN 37247
(615) 741-0213

TEXAS
Dept of Human Services
Health Care Services
P.O. Box 149030
Austin, TX 78714
(512) 450-3050

UTAH
Division of Health Care Financing
Utah Dept of Health
P.O. Box 16580
Salt Lake City, UT 84116
(801) 538-6151

VERMONT
Dept of Social Welfare
Vermont Agency of Human Services
103 S. Main Street
Waterbury, VT 05676
(802) 241-2880

VIRGIN ISLANDS
Dept of Human Services
Barbel Plaza South
St. Thomas, VI 00802
(809) 774-0930

VIRGINIA
Virginia Dept of Medical Assistance Services
600 E. Broad Street, Suite 1300
Richmond, VA 23212
(804) 786-7933

WASHINGTON
Medicaid Recipient Assistance & Information
617 8th Avenue SE
Olympia, WA 98504
1-800-562-3022

WEST VIRGINIA
Division of Medical Care
West Virginia Dept of Human Services
State Capital Complex
Building 6, Room 717B
Charleston, WV 25305
(304) 348-8990

WISCONSIN
Division of Health
Wisconsin Dept of Health & Social Services
P.O. Box 309
Madison, WI 53701
(608) 266-2522

WYOMING
Medical Assistance Services
Dept of Health & Social Services
6101 Yellowstone
Cheyenne, WY 82002
(307) 777-7531

State Insurance Commissions

ALABAMA
Commissioner of Insurance
135 South Union Street #160
P.O. Box 303351
Montgomery, AL 36130-3351
(334) 241-4101

ALASKA
Director of Insurance
P.O. Box 110805
Juneau, AK 99811
(907) 465-2515

AMERICAN SAMOA
Office of the Governor
Pago Pago, AS 96796
(684) 633-4116

ARIZONA
Director of Insurance
2910 N. 44th Street
Suite 210
Phoenix, AZ 85018
(602) 912-8456

ARKANSAS
Insurance Commissioner
University Tower Building.
1123 South University Avenue
Suite 400
Little Rock, AR 72204
(501) 686-2909

CALIFORNIA
Insurance Commissioner
45 Fremont Street, 23rd Floor
San Francisco, CA 94105
(415) 904-5410

COLORADO
Commissioner of Insurance
1560 Broadway, Suite 850
Denver, CO 80202
(303) 894-7499

CONNECTICUT
Insurance Commissioner
Insurance Department
165 Capitol Avenue
State Office Building, Room 425
P.O. Box 816
Hartford, CT 06142
(203) 297-3802

DELAWARE
Insurance Commission
Rodney Building
841 Silver Lake Boulevard
Dover, DE 19904
(302) 739-4251

DISTRICT OF COLUMBIA
Commissioner of Insurance
Department of Consumer and
Regulatory Affairs
One Judiciary Square
441 4th Street, NW
8th Floor North
Washington, DC 20001
(202) 727-8000

FLORIDA
Insurance Commission
State Treasurer's Office
State Capitol
Plaza Level Eleven
Tallahassee, FL 32399-0300
(904) 922-3100

GEORGIA
Commissioner of Insurance
7th Floor, West Tower
Floyd Building
2 Martin Luther King, Jr Drive
Atlanta, GA 30334
(404) 656-2056

GUAM
P.O. Box 2796
855 West Marine Drive
Agana, GU 96910
011-671-477-1040

HAWAII
Insurance Commissioner
Department of Commerce and
Consumer Affairs
P.O. Box 3614
Honolulu, HI 96811
(808) 586-2790

IDAHO
Director of Insurance
500 S. 10th Street
P.O. Box 83720
Boise, ID 83720
(208) 334-4250

ILLINOIS
Director of Insurance
State of Illinois
320 West Washington Street
4th Floor
Springfield, IL 62767
(217) 782-4515

INDIANA
Commissioner of Insurance
311 West Washington Street
Suite 300
Indianapolis, IN 46204-2787
(317) 232-3520

IOWA
Commissioner of Insurance
Lucas State Office Building
6th Floor
Des Moines, IA 50319
(515) 281-5523

KANSAS
Commissioner of Insurance
420 S.W. 9th Street
Topeka, KS 66612
(913) 296-3071

KENTUCKY
Insurance Commissioner
215 West Main Street
P.O. Box 517
Frankfort, KY 40602
(502) 564-6027

LOUISIANA
Commissioner of Insurance
950 N. 5th Street
P.O. Box 94214
Baton Rouge, LA 70804-9214
(504) 342-5423

MAINE
Superintendent of Insurance
State Office Building
State House, Station 34
Augusta, ME 04333
(207) 582-8707

MARYLAND
Insurance Commissioner
501 St. Paul Place
(Stanbalt Bldg)
7th Floor-South
Baltimore, MD 21202
(410) 333-2521

MASSACHUSETTS
Commissioner of Insurance
470 Atlantic Avenue
Boston, MA 02210
(617) 521-7794

MICHIGAN
Insurance Commissioner
P.O. Box 30220
Lansing, MI 48909
611 West Ottawa Street
2nd Floor
North Lansing, MI 48933
(517) 373-9273

MINNESOTA
Commissioner of Commerce
133 East 7th Street
St Paul, MN 55101
(612) 296-6694

MISSISSIPPI
Commissioner of Insurance
1804 Walter Sillers Bld
P.O. Box 79
Jackson, MS 39205
(601) 359-3569

MISSOURI
Director, Department of Insurance
301 West High Street, 6 North
P.O. Box 690
Jefferson City, MO 65102-0690
(314) 751-4126

MONTANA
Commissioner of Insurance
126 North Sanders
Mitchell Building
Room 270
P.O. Box 4009
Helena, MT 59604
(406) 444-2040

NEBRASKA
Director of Insurance
Terminal Building
941 O Street, Suite 400
Lincoln, NE 68508
(402) 471-2201

NEVADA
Commissioner of Insurance
Capitol Complex
1685 Hot Springs Road, Suite 152
Carson City, NV 89710
(702) 687-4270

NEW HAMPSHIRE
Insurance Commissioner
169 Manchester Street
Concord, NH 03301
(603) 271-2261

NEW JERSEY
Commissioner of Insurance
20 West State Street
CN325
Trenton, NJ 08625
(609) 292-5350

NEW MEXICO
Superintendent of Insurance
Pera Bldg.
P.O. Drawer 1269
Santa Fe, NM 87504-1269
(505) 827-4500

NEW YORK
Superintendent of Insurance
160 West Broadway
New York, NY 10013
(212) 602-0429

NORTH CAROLINA
Commissioner of Insurance
430 North Salisbury Street
Dobbs Building
Raleigh, NC 27603
P.O. Box 26387
Raleigh, NC 27611
(919) 733-7349

NORTH DAKOTA
Commissioner of Insurance
Capitol Bldg., 600 East Boulevard
5th Floor
Bismarck, ND 58505
(701) 328-2440

OHIO
Director of Insurance
2100 Stella Court
Columbus, OH 43215
(614) 644-2651

OKLAHOMA
Insurance Commissioner
1901 North Walnut
Oklahoma City, OK 73105
P.O. Box 53408
Oklahoma City, OK 73152-3404
(405) 521-2828

OREGON
Insurance Commissioner
440 Labor & Industries Bldg
Salem, OR 97310
(503) 378-4100

PENNSYLVANIA
Insurance Commissioner
Strawberry Square
13th Floor
Harrisburg, PA 17120
(717) 783-0442

PUERTO RICO
Fernandez Juncos Station
P.O. Box 8330
Santurce, PR 00910
(809) 722-8686

RHODE ISLAND
Director of Business Regulation
and Insurance Commissioner
State of Rhode Island
233 Richmond Street, Suite 233
Providence, RI 02903-4237
(401) 277-2223

SOUTH CAROLINA
Chief Insurance Commissioner
1612 Marion Street
Columbia, SC 29201
P.O. Box 100105
Columbia, SC 29202-3105
(803) 737-6160

SOUTH DAKOTA
Director of Insurance
Insurance Building
910 East Sioux Avenue
Pierre, SD 57501
(605) 773-3563

TENNESSEE
Commissioner of Commerce and
Insurance
Volunteer Plaza
500 James Robertson Parkway
Nashville, TN 37243
(615) 741-2241

TEXAS
Commissioner of Insurance
333 Guadalupe Street
Austin, TX 78701-1998
(512) 463-6464

UTAH
Commissioner of Insurance
3110 State Office Building
Salt Lake City, UT 84114
(801) 538-3804

VERMONT
Commissioner of Banking,
Insurance and Securities
89 Main Street, Drawer 20
Montpelier, VT 05602
(802) 828-3301

VIRGINIA
Commissioner of Insurance
Tyler Building
P.O. Box 1157
Richmond, VA 23209
(804) 371-9694

VIRGIN ISLANDS
Kongens Gade #18
St. Thomas, VI 00802
(809) 774-2991

WASHINGTON
Insurance Commissioner
Insurance Building, AQ21
P.O. Box 40255
Olympia, WA 98504
(360) 753-7301

WEST VIRGINIA
Insurance Commissioner
2019 Washington Street, East
Charleston, WV 25305
(304) 558-3354

WISCONSIN
Commissioner of Insurance
121 East Wilson Street
P.O. Box 7873
Madison, WI 53707
(608) 266-0102

WYOMING
Insurance Commissioner
Herschler Building
122 West 25th Street, 3 East
Cheyenne, WY 82002
(307) 777-7401

Finding a lawyer

- A free booklet, *Questions and Answers When Looking for an Elder Law Attorney,* can be obtained by sending a *stamped, self–addressed envelope* to:

  National Academy of Elder Law Attorneys
  655 N. Alvernon Way, Suite 108
  Tucson, AZ 85711

- Referrals: For a name or names of an elder law attorney in your state, see the form at the end of this chapter.

Books for caregivers

- *How to Care for Your Aging Parents: A Handbook for Adult Children*
  Nora Jean Levin
  The kind of short guide that should be in every family's bookcase. 103 pages, $5.95.

  Storm King Press
  Box 3566
  Washington, DC 20007

- *The Elder Law Handbook: A Legal and Financial Survival Guide for Caregivers and Seniors*
  Peter J. Strauss and Nancy M. Lederman

  Facts on File
  Available in bookstores

- *You and Your Aging Parent: A Family Guide to Emotional, Physical and Financial Problems*
  Barbara Silverstone and Helen Kandel Hyman
  A helpful guide through the maze of emotional and practical problems of caregiving. 351 pages, $14.95.

  Pantheon Books
  Available in bookstores

- *How to Survive Your Aging Parent... So You and They Can Enjoy Life.*
  Bernard H. Shulman, M.D. and Raeann Berman
  A compassionate look at the frustrations, anxieties and rewards of caregiving. 192 pages,$10.95.

  Surrey Books
  101 East Erie Street
  Chicago, IL 60611

• *Talking With Your Aging Parents*
Mark A. Edinberg
How to communicate with your parents about troublesome subjects like nursing homes, legal and financial matters, and death. 220 pages, $9.95.

Shambhala Publications
300 Massachusetts Avenue
Boston, MA 02115

Help for caregivers

• Children of Aging Parents (CAPS)
A national clearinghouse for caregivers to the elderly and for professionals in the field of aging. Support groups, a hotline, a newsletter and more.
Membership: Individual, $15.
Professional or organizational, $25.

2761 Trenton Road
Levittown, PA 19056
(215) 945–6900

Especially for seniors

- *American Guidance for Seniors*
  Ken Skala
  You can take advantage of the many state, federal and private programs for the elderly but only if you know about them. This is an indispensible handbook of benefits, entitlements, and assistance for Americans over age sixty. An excellent resource. 531 pages, $15.95 plus $4.00 postage and handling.

  American Guidance, Inc.
  6231 Leesburg Pike, Suite 305
  Falls Church, VA 22044

- *How to Keep Control of Your Life After 50: A Guide for Your Legal, Medical, and Financial Well–Being*
  Offers the knowledge and the tools necessary for elderly people to get what they want—in their medical treatment, their finances, and in making important decisions. 428 pages, $17.95.

  Macmillan Publishing Company
  100 Front Street
  Box 500
  Riverside, NJ 08075–7500

- *ElderLaw News*
  A readable four–page quarterly newsletter presenting elderly law developments and estate planning techniques for the general public.

  ElderLaw News
  101 Arch Street
  Boston, MA 02110
  $15 for a one–year subscription

On assisted–living communities

Continuing Care Accreditation Commission
1129 20th Street NW, Suite 400
Washington, DC 20036
(202) 828-9439

Assisted Living Facilities Association
9411 Lee Highway
Fairfax, VA 20031
(703) 691-8100

For professionals

- *The Medicaid Planning Handbook*
  Alexander A. Bove, Jr., Esq.
  Two versions, one for professionals, the other for lay people. *Covers Massachusetts only*. $23 plus $3.50 for postage and handling.

  Ormand Sacker Press
  P.O. Box 4526
  Boston, MA 02101

- *Aging and the Law*
  Peter Strauss, Robert Wolf and Dana Shilling
  An excellent comprehensive resource for professionals—lawyers, accountants, insurance consultants, physicians, social workers, gerontologists. 912 pages, $100.

  Commerce Clearing House, Inc.
  4025 West Peterson Avenue
  Chicago, IL 60646
  1–800–248–3248

- *The ElderLaw Report*
  An in–depth, up–to–date monthly report on legal developments and planning techniques that the elderly–law professional needs to know. 8 to 12 pages, $89 for one year.

The ElderLaw Report
Little, Brown and Company
Law Division
34 Beacon Street
Boston, MA 02108

Agencies

- Your Office of Elder Affairs (in your phone book under government)
- Your state Division of Insurance (see preceding chapter)
- Your local Department of Public Welfare (the name varies state by state. It may also be called the Department of Social Services, the Department of Economic Security, or any of a handful of other similar names. See preceding chapter)

Insurance

- *A Shopper's Guide to Long–Term Care Insurance*
  A booklet of basic non–critical information including a helpful policy comparison checklist. First copy free.

  National Association of Insurance Commissioners
  120 West 12th Street
  Kansas City, MO 64105

- *A.M. Best's Insurance Report*
  Perhaps the most widely used reference of this sort. It evaluates insurance companies' relative financial strength using six ratings: Superior (A+), Excellent (A or A–), Very Good (B+), Good (B or B–), Fairly Good (C), or Fair (C or C–). You can look up any company by going to your local library. Your librarian can direct you to two other rating sources, Standard and Poor's and Moody's, as well.

- *Long–Term Care — Solving the Need*
  Joseph Pulitano and Attorney Harley Gordon
  A comprehensive, self–study, continuing–education course for insurance agents. Approved for CE credit in most states. 120 pages. $34.95 + $25 grading fee.

  Senior Planning Group Publications
  214 Lincoln Street, Suite 110
  Allston, MA 02134
  1-800-LTC-ATTY

Books on the issues

- *Risking Old Age in America*
  Richard J. Margolis
  A Families USA Foundation Book
  A beautiful, warm book that puts human faces on the facts and statistics of aging. If the issues facing the elderly don't particularly interest you, reading

this book will raise your consciousness and move you to the heart. Part sociological treatise, part touching narrative, this work is an example of how a gifted writer can make any subject compelling. 202 pages. $14.95 plus $3.00 for postage and handling.

Westview Press
5500 Central Avenue
Boulder, CO 80301
1–800–456–1995

- *Critical Issues: A National Health System for America*
edited by Stuart M. Butler and Edmund F. Haislmaier
A strategy to make adequate, affordable health care available to every American. 127 pages, $8.00.

The Heritage Foundation
Publications Department
214 Massachusetts Avenue, NE
Washington, DC 20002
(202) 546–4400

• *Caring for the Disabled Elderly: Who Will Pay?*
Alice M. Rivlin and Joshua M. Wiener
An examination of possible solutions to the problem of financing long–term care. 318 pages.

Brookings Institution
1775 Massachusetts Avenue, NW
Washington, DC 20036

For corporations

• The Dependent Care Connection
Employee *counseling services*
A national child care and elder care information/referral/counseling service providing assistance to workers through employer participation.

Dependent Care Connection
PO Box 2783
Westport, CT 06880
(203) 226–2680

Support services

- Alzheimer's Disease & Related Disorders Association

  A source for referrals to local chapters and support groups.

  70 East Lake Street
  Suite 600
  Chicago, IL 60601
  1–800–621–0379
  In Illinois, 1–800–527–6037

- Arthritis Foundation

  A source for referrals to local chapters, support groups, doctors and clinics.

  1314 Spring Street, NW
  Atlanta, GA 30309
  1–800–283–7800

- National Parkinson Foundation

  1501 NW 9th Avenue
  Miami, FL 33136
  (305) 547–6666
  1–800–3274545

- Health Information Center

  A source for information and help for a wide variety of health problems. A good starting place for referrals.

  PO Box 1133
  Washington, DC 20013
  1–800–336–4797

Health hotlines

There are at least 300 health–related hotlines that provide assistance free of charge. People coping with Alzheimer's, arthritis, cancer, heart disease, osteoporosis or many other health problems can find help in a directory of health hotlines. To receive a copy, write to:

Health Hotlines
Public Information Office
National Library of Medicine
Bethesda, MD 20894

Mail to: **Financial Strategies Press, Inc.**
15 Broad Street, #700
Boston, MA 02109

Update notification

Medicaid laws change frequently. This means that we will be updating this book in the future. If you would like to be notified of updated editions, please provide your contact information. There is no charge for this service. We do not share our mailing list with other companies.

Name ____________________

Number and street ____________________

City/town ____________________

State ____________ Zip ____________ Phone ____________

Metropolitan area or nearest large city: ____________________

Request for referral

☐ *Check this box if you would like to find an attorney who is familiar with the field of elderly law. We will send you one or more names and addresses of attorneys in your area whom you can call for help.*

To obtain the referral service, please enclose the fee of $15.00 and sign the release on the reverse side. Allow up to three weeks for a response.

We will try to give you names close to your address; however, this may not always be possible.

Area of interest: *(Circle one or more)*

1. Estate planning, including wills and trusts
2. Guardianship/conservatorship
3. Medicaid planning

Please read the following carefully:

This service is offered to provide additional resources to readers of this book in the form of elder law attorneys. Financial Strategies Press, Inc., and Harley Gordon do not receive any referral fee or other compensation of any nature from the attorneys whose names are given out. The author has taken reasonable steps to assure that the lawyers whose names are provided through this service are experienced in the area of elderly law. No warranty, express or implied, is made as to their competency.

Please read and sign:

I agree to take reasonable steps to verify the competency of any attorney I engage. By signing below, I release Financial Strategies Press, Inc., and the author of this book from any liability that might arise from this referral.

Signed: ______________________ Date: ______________________

INDEX

NOTES

NOTES